A TREASURY OF
TIPS FOR
WRITERS

By the American Society of Journalists and Authors

Edited by Marvin Weisbord

 Cincinnati, Ohio

Second printing, 1969

Third printing, 1975

Fourth printing, 1979

First Paperback Printing, 1981

Library of Congress Cataloging in Publication Data

American Society of Journalists and Authors.
 A treasury of tips for writers.

 Edition for 1965 by the society under its earlier name: Society of Magazine Writers.
 1. Authorship. I. Weisbord, Marvin Ross. II. Society of Magazine Writers. A treasury of tips
for writers. III. Title.
PN147.S574 1979   808'.025   79-11859
ISBN 0-89879-050-6

Writer's Digest Books
9933 Alliance Road, Cincinnati, Ohio 45242

TABLE OF CONTENTS

Two Idea Mines . . . Read the Ads . . . Show What You Can Do . . . Changing Ideas in Midstream . . . Ideas for Top Magazines Come from Daily Papers . . . Watch for New Ideas in Your Interviews . . . You Live Article Ideas . . . Seeking Ideas at Club and Association Meetings . . . How Many People are Involved? . . . Anticipate What Magazines Will Need . . . If at First You Don't Succeed . . . Developing Your Automatic Idea Alert

Always Ask — The Answer is Often "Yes" . . . You Can Get a *Reader's Digest Index* . . . Research Help from Radio Hams . . . Ideas and Research from Government Agency Reports . . . More on Governmental Sources . . . Seek Out Multiple Sources . . . Some People Like Writing Letters . . . Time, Incorporated Provides Free Tearsheets . . . Getting Information by Mail . . . Free Copies of Congressional Hearings . . . Utilizing Government Public Information Officers . . . Sources on Military Stories . . . Subscribing to

. . . Some Tips for Newspaper People Who Want to Write for Magazines . . . Keeping a Work Sheet . . . Keep Track of All Activities on a Single File Card . . . Cost Accounting Your Time . . . Special Tips from a Columnist . . . Don't Spurn a Specialty . . . Research that Pays Off.

A TREASURY OF TIPS FOR WRITERS

Introduction

In 1948 four nonfiction writers — Murray Teigh Bloom, Phil Gustafson, Beatrice Schapper and Jack Harrison Pollack — met at the Author's Guild and found that they liked to talk shop. Their luncheon gab-fest grew by osmosis, absorbing other shop-talkers and, as inevitably as Parkinson's Law, the Society of Magazine Writers was born.

Today, SMW has 220 members, all professionals, all established writers for national magazines. The Society itself sponsors editorial awards, dispenses foundation grants and works to elevate the standards and rewards of magazine journalism.

Creeping institutionalization, however, has not cut off the flow of shoptalk. At least once a year SMW holds a craft session as part of the monthly dinner meeting at the Overseas Press Club in New York City. When 50 or 60 writers get together to discuss ideas, research, good and bad agents and editors, and the not-so-subtle balance between art and income, then lightning crackles in the room. To magazine writers, shoptalk restores tired blood. Whether we specialize in medicine, money, travel, civil rights, people or politics, we are bound in fellowship by our problems: how to dig out facts and opinions, how to work with editors, how to keep ideas flowing, how to drive oneself to the typewriter rather than to drink.

Most writers—unlike doctors, lawyers, or accountants—are self-taught. No school certifies us, no board examines us, and we get no minimum wage. A writer's license to practice derives from what he's written and sold. As a result, most writers have an extraordinary respect for experience and tend to be generous in sharing it. Nearly every writer has cribbed tricks of the trade from somebody else. Hal Higdon, for example, picked up a way of organizing articles from Bernie Asbell. Frank Cameron adopted a planning system invented by Frank Taylor. Jamie Maxtone Graham learned the fruits of collaboration from Wilbur Cross. Alden Todd once remarked that Al Toffler taught him to write query letters. And I, having been in and out of libraries for years, finally picked up some efficient library habits from Alden Todd. In short, most writers cheerfully climb on each other's shoulders.

In this book 86 seasoned writers have tried to explain some of their favorite techniques. This is a compendium of habits, tricks, devices, tips, and gimmicks which professional writers and researchers use. Some were learned, some invented, some stumbled upon by accident. None are patented. Nor are any foolproof. You must experiment for yourself to decide whether any technique suggested here will work for you. Nevertheless, we invite you to climb on our shoulders. Whether you intend to write articles, books, theses, term papers, or factual reports of any kind, chances are you'll find in these pages that somebody who has traveled the route before can steer you around the potholes and pitfalls of writing.

The book is arranged into a dozen chapters, progressing from ideas to research to sources to writing to business problems. A technique may be a single-paragraph hint or it may be a two-page essay. Our writers were given the widest latitude in subject matter, length and number of items to submit. Each was asked to write something he had learned that might be useful to others.

The oldest and most revered advice to article writers is "study the magazine." Editors tell you this so you won't waste your time and theirs sending "Newton's Laws of Motion" to *Redbook* or "Twelve

Ways to Increase the Value of Your Home" to *The New Yorker* or a batch of pictures with captions to *Reader's Digest.* This advice is basic, but it's only a start. Most of what follows here *cannot* be learned by reading magazines, for the good writer tells you only what he wants you to know. He doesn't explain how he ran down the apt quote, the sparkling anecdote, the obscure statistic, the hard-to-reach interviewee. He omits the number of books read, newspapers scanned, phone calls made, hours of sleep lost and aspirins swallowed. His published article is like a new car in the showroom — bright and polished, with little evidence of the arduous work that went into it.

But there is more to writing than the finished product. Lord Macaulay, the English historian and essayist, read a score of books to write a single sentence, and he once traveled 100 miles so he could describe a scene in one line. But Macaulay's genius lay in his ability, as Allan Nevins put it, "to thrust the non-essentials out of sight. He was interested in the finished structure and did not bother his readers with a view of the scaffolding used to put it up or the shavings and litter discarded in the process."

This is a book about the scaffolding, shavings and litter. We believe this is the part of writing which can be taught and learned. You will see soon enough that there is more than one way to find and draw out an interviewee, just as there's more than one way to write a good lead. The method you choose must fit your own habits, temperament and aims. Bill Lederer, co-author with Eugene Burdick of *The Ugly American,* summed it up in a note with his contribution to this book. "What is important," he wrote, "is that all of us *try* to help others in this writing business."

In a work with so many authors it seems superfluous to remark that without the generous gift of time and energy by each, there would have been no book. But especial thanks and acknowledgment are due Frank Thomas, Hal Higdon and Gerald Walker for their efforts in planning this project, and certainly to Alden Todd, who not only helped organize the book but who, with his sharp pencil, saved us now and again from looking a little bit foolish. Finally on the *Writer's Digest* end, thanks are due Richard Rosenthal and SMW-member Allan Eckert for their painstaking and good-humored editorial work.

Marvin Weisbord,
Merion Station, Pa.
June — 1965

Introduction
to the Second Edition

The American Society of Journalists and Authors, now 570 members strong, continues the traditions of the Society of Magazine Writers. The Society's name was changed to reflect the broadened interests of its members, who still write for magazines but who also write books in ever-increasing numbers. The Society, headquartered in New York with five regional chapters, still works steadily to raise the standards and rewards of magazine journalism; it applies the same efforts in the realm of book publishing. ASJA's Code of Ethics and Fair Standards, Model Letter of Agreement for magazine articles, and Position Statement on Work Made for Hire have all had a positive effect on the industry, improving conditions for all writers. And its periodic Conscience-in-Media Award recognizes distinctive contributions by any journalist in any medium.

Our unifying interest remains, however, the craft of nonfiction and the constant refinement of that craft. Our annual writers' conferences, currently held in New York, Southern California, and Madison, Wisconsin, are designed to share our wealth of knowledge.

This book is also a means of sharing our skills and experience with you. The first edition of *A Treasury of Tips for Writers* became a classic in its fifteen-year life. This revised and updated version, in which factual material has been brought in line with the realities of the 1980s, should prove even more valuable.

This second edition was edited by Terry Morris, skilled professional writer and past president of ASJA. The bibliography was prepared by Alden Todd, teacher of research techniques and author of *Finding Facts Fast.* To both, our thanks.

Grace W. Weinstein
President, ASJA
January 1981

Chapter One

ARTICLE IDEAS

Two Idea Mines:
The Congressional Record and Out-of-Town Newspapers

As an off-beat source for ideas, I've found the *Congressional Record* very helpful. It's published daily and if you're lucky you can get on your Congressman's free list; otherwise, it runs about $18 for a year's subscription. The *Record* is published each day Congress is in session and contains a wealth of information. In addition to being a transcript of what is discussed in the House and Senate, the *Record* is packed with speeches, reprints of articles and local news clips that can be a good source of ideas. Also, you'll find it suggests experts who may be willing to join you in by-lining a piece. For example, my first sale to *True* grew out of a speech made by an Ohio senator, lambasting civil defense. On the basis of the views he expressed in the speech (recorded in full in the *Record*), I persuaded him to do an "as-told-to" called "The U. S. Should Scrap Its Civil Defense." His speech had not been carried in the Chicago newspapers and I wouldn't have known of it if I hadn't read the *Record*.

Similarly, another story I did for *True,* an exposé of the Bird-man of Alcatraz myth, grew out of a report by a Missouri senator entered in the *Record* in connection with his job as chairman of the penitentiaries committee. In addition to providing good leads on ideas, the *Record* frequently prints valuable statistical compilations on a wide range of subjects that are hard to find elsewhere and can easily be clipped. The *Record,* incidentally, is indexed and can be checked at any depository library.

Another source of ideas, particularly for the writer based outside New York City who wants to specialize in covering the area of the country around him, is Sunday newspapers. When time permits, I read some 17 Sunday newspapers from 14 Midwestern states — papers regularly on file at the Chicago library. Sunday is the day most features are carried and from the papers you can get leads on little-known people or events that are locally centered but which may make good reading in a national magazine. For instance, in reading a Pittsburgh paper I learned of a new company opening up there to specialize in "cleaning up" after accidents involving radioactive materials. The story was not carried by wire services or any other newspaper. However, with considerable expansion it developed into a good piece for *Popular Mechanics.*   *—Charles Remsberg*

Read the Ads

Article ideas usually generate themselves. Sometimes, however, you dry up. When this happens I simply pull out about 50 back issue magazines and thumb through them, concentrating primarily on the ads. Although editors protest loudly that they're not influenced by advertisers, it's a good idea to know where the revenue is coming from. I once sold an article about "learning by mail" to a magazine with lots of correspondence school ads; another about drug research to a magazine heavy with drug company blurbs. Reading the ads doesn't always work — but it's better than staring at the wall.

—S. L. Englebardt

Show What You Can Do

It's a magazine you've never written for and you have, after a good many abortive phone calls, been given an appointment with the managing editor, no less. And what happens? A few initial pleasantries and then you stumble over your words in an effort to convince him that this article you want to do on a forgotten Civil

War hero is the very thing for his magazine. But the editor has hardly heard of you; he doesn't know your style, your past achievements or the scope of your work. You might be just a would-be freelance who can't write well at all. Then again, you could be the Real McCoy. You have about a half-hour to convince him you can deliver what he needs. How best can you put across yourself and your work?

My own system, based on an idea cribbed from my collaborator, Wilbur Cross, is to carry in my briefcase half a dozen copies of my List of Subjects. It runs to five foolscap pages, single-spaced on a friend's IBM Executive. We did a stencil and the cost came to less than a dime per copy. Each of the 90 subjects — some already in completed manuscript form, others no more than ideas backed up by a growing file of news clippings — is given two or three lines. The Civil War hero is there and you point him out to the editor. He glances at it and promptly goes back to page one. "Hey, this is a good scheme," he says, echoing what I've heard editors say time and again. "I wish more writers did it." A sharp editor can get through the immense list in half an hour, but suddenly . . .

"This ancestor of Sir Alec Douglas-Home — 'the greatest medium of all time, fantastic feats of levitation and spookery' — sounds interesting. Tell me more about it," or, perhaps, "Why don't you send me an outline?"

My two or three lines are really outlines of outlines. And I take care *not* to split the list into subject categories. An imaginative editor of a man's magazine can detect in a feminine subject masculine aspects that the author never dreamed of. Thus,

> THE TALE OF SAWNEY BEANE: *story of the 16th Century Scottish cannibal who, with his family of 46 incestuously begotten descendants, lived in a cave for 25 years and killed and consumed well over 1,000 travelers. . . .*

happens to come right next door to

> THE COMPLEAT ANGEL: *article extolling, for women, the virtues of fishing. . . .*

I am not saying that Sawney Beane will necessarily appear in *McCall's,* but you never know. Even in such a short space there is sometimes room for a tantalizing anecdote:

> *HANDCUFFS: story on Hiatt and Co. of Birmingham, one of the world's three handcuff manufacturers. "I know Houdini's secret," said the managing director, "but I'm not telling anyone. It wouldn't be good for trade."*

When an article has been written and bought, it does not disappear from the list. "To be published in *Sports Illustrated*" or "*Atlantic,* April 1982" are words which will not be lost to the eye of an observant editor.

I don't pretend that the list is read thoroughly wherever I take or send it, and I am well aware that half the copies soon end up in the trash basket. But, as a way of giving an indication of your status and abilities and of selling *yourself,* it has much to commend it. And sometimes you can tell you're on the right track when at the end of a talk with an editor he says, "Do you mind if I keep this?"

—J. A. Maxtone Graham

Changing Ideas in Midstream

Sometimes, of course, in the midst of researching an article, circumstances change and you discover that the article you planned to deliver cannot be done exactly that way. This does not mean that you will lose your assignment. If you contact the editor he may well agree with you that another approach will make an even better story. However, the businesslike writer lets the editor know about this change before he makes it.

Here is an example from my own experience. I was given an assignment from *American Weekly* to write an article on the Aegean Islands. The editor and I agreed it would be ideal if I could find a young American couple living on one of the Greek islands who could serve as an example to other Americans seeking a beautiful "escape island." I found, instead, a most interesting, charming, middle-aged American painter.

I instantly cabled the editor, described the situation and asked his opinion. He cabled back that I should "move ahead." If he had not, I would have continued to look until I found the kind of couple we had discussed.

As it turned out, the painter was ideal. He had many friends and through the story of the painter I was able to bring in anecdotes and material about many young couples who lived in the Islands — and so we ended up in a way with what we originally wanted, plus something new. —*Amelia Lobsenz*

Ideas for Top Magazines Come from the Daily Papers

I'm constantly on the lookout for ideas that will make strong dramatic narrative pieces. Most of my ideas come right off pages one and two of the daily newspapers. A paragraph, a sentence, even a phrase has told me there might be a good story behind the headline. These stories are best if you can focus upon one person or a few people involved in a personal kind of "hell"—a crime, hurricane, mine disaster or the like. Such stories usually attract a strong reader response because they have the elements of "there-but-for-the-grace-of-God-go-I." They can fail, too, if you are trapped with people who are not articulate or likeable or people who simply do not feel the drama that was apparent to you.

Here are a few examples of article ideas plucked from newspapers:

A soccer game riot at Lima, Peru, in which 300 persons were killed. The idea came from page one of the *New York Times* and sold to *Reader's Digest*.

The hijacking over El Paso of a Boeing 707 airliner. This made page one of all daily newspapers and became my piece in *True*.

An escaped convict who voluntarily surrendered after 27 years. I learned about him on page two of the *New York Herald Tribune* and sold the piece to *The Saturday Evening Post*. —*Joseph P. Blank*

Watch for New Ideas in Your Interviews

Contrary to some professional statements, I find telephone interviewing successful, as I can be taking notes at a furious pace, page after page, though still sounding perfectly casual as I encourage the interviewee.

While gathering information for "How to Enjoy Hot Weather" for *This Week,* I phoned a Washington, D.C. weather bureau chief. I sought facts about the pre-air conditioning formulae for excusing employees when the temperature was so much and the humidity so drippy much. But the man wandered off the subject into anecdotes about the automatic weather-dialing system, then fairly new.

Recognizing the charm of his little stories, I made rapid notes, afterwards storing them in my Ideas File. (Of course, it would make recovery easier to have separate files on appealing subjects, but I chuck ideas together until a project jells.)

Two years later, "Forecasts at Your Fingertip" was a *Saturday Evening Post* natural because the weather-dialing was new in Philadelphia. I went back to my precious anecdotes and telephoned the same chief. He couldn't produce a single additional anecdote! Either his mood had changed or he had told his all during the first telephone interview on another subject. But I had what *Satevepost* needed, thanks to my habit of writing down anything good which comes my way.   —*Ruth Boyer Scott*

You Live Article Ideas

Here's my personal secret for finding article ideas: I like to say that I support my family but this isn't altogether true; in a certain respect, my family supports me. We have children, a house in the suburbs—and problems.

Every day in the week we *live* magazine article ideas. I figure that if a problem puzzles our little basic unit of civilization, our little family, then perhaps it may also puzzle all the other little units that make up America.

I also figure that if I discover a solution to my problem—and if this solution is valid—many other persons would be interested in applying it to themselves.

I cannot count the number of articles I have mined from my own family problems, as well as those of my friends and neighbors. And these are not likely to be stereotyped problems, either. One of the most successful articles I ever wrote was sparked by a living room discussion at a small party. One fellow complained that his wife wasn't preparing breakfast for him. It was a kidding argument, of course, but with just a smallish sting involved, enough to give it a bit of interest and impact. So I made an article out of wives who don't prepare breakfast for their husbands.

Since you never run out of problems, neither do you run out of salable ideas. Families with children develop many problems to solve, with the fascinations, complexities and headaches that accompany them. To cite a few: "The Great American Pet Boom," "Our Kids Are Too Rich," and "Don't Rush Your Daughter Into Marriage."

From observations of my own family, it is just one step away to observe others. In my own suburban community there occurred a suicide, a case of a severely handicapped child, a dramatic auto accident and many other incidents, each of which could feasibly be translated into a meaningful and instructive magazine article. With this family idea going for me, probably the only time I'll ever run out of ideas will be when I go into a retirement home for old magazine writers. Even then, there's always geriatrics.

—Lester David

Seeking Ideas at Club and Association Meetings

Don't overlook meetings of clubs and associations as possibilities for inspiring good article ideas. At various intervals throughout the year most of us attend meetings of one kind or another. Not all of these will inspire an article but, over a period of time, enough of them will to make this a source of ideas which shouldn't be entirely overlooked.

If you spend all your writing time at the typewriter you may run dry or fall into a rut. Conversely, if you spend too much time at meetings you won't produce much copy. Yet, as many other professional writers do, I continue to seek article material at such meetings.

The decision of whether or not you should attend a particular meeting will come easier if you can answer "yes" to one or both of the following questions:

1. Is this meeting likely to produce an article directly?

2. Will this meeting have value for my family or myself, even though no immediate article appears probable?

Sometimes such meetings will provide the basis for an article which could not otherwise have been written. A case in point involved a famous man who was the speaker at my child's school but who would never allow himself to be interviewed for an article. Yet, the notes I took as he spoke to the parents enabled me to build a major article for *Better Homes & Gardens*.

Next time a meeting looms, answer those two questions for yourself to decide whether to attend or to stay at your typewriter.

—*Ruth Boyer Scott*

How Many People Are Involved?

Normally I don't believe in "don'ts" for the writer. However, there is one mistake nearly every news reporter or feature writer makes when he first starts trying for the magazines. It might be called "Ripley-itis." A two-headed calf or a five-legged toad become spot news in your own city or area. Fascinating? Not to that managing editor sitting in his New York office. To him it means nothing except, perhaps, a fleeting sadness when he has to turn thumbs down on the enthusiasm of one more amateur.

The fact that an incident or event is a story in your town, for your paper, unfortunately does not signify national appeal. *But,* if the event highlights a national trend or can be developed to disclose something the readers from coast to coast would want to know, then you're on the right scent. Your job becomes one of broadening the coverage, comparing it to past events, projecting it to the future as it may affect any reader. In other words, you have to beef it up and make of it something with as much impact for the reader in San Diego as the one in Kokomo.

Thus, the bombing of a laundry in Chicago means little to a national magazine . . . but when Cosa Nostra mobsters start taking over a lot of legitimate or pseudo-legitimate businesses, when they begin branching out at various points on the national scene, *then* you have the interest the national magazine needs. So when the above incidents actually did occur, Bill Davidson met the challenge and provided a major story for *The Saturday Evening Post.*

Virtually the same line of reasoning holds where individuals are concerned. A nice little old lady who feeds cats is just that and nothing more . . . unless her name happens to be Greta Garbo, whereupon it assumes national significance. Bear in mind that nationally significant people live everywhere across the country.

The moral: think as big as you can when writing for mass magazines. Ask yourself, "How many people are really involved?"
—*Charles W. White*

Anticipate What Magazines Will Need

Editors often get desperate for halfway fresh article ideas that can be tied in with holidays; i.e., Mother's Day, Father's Day, Independence Day. Line up the holidays at least six or seven months in advance and see if you can come up with some fresh ideas.

Very important! Keep the ideas or suggestions flowing. Try not to let a week go by without sending out a few ideas. Even if you are working on assignments, continue sending out suggestions, making phone calls to editors, maintaining your vital contact with editorial staffs.

Remember, too, you can never know for sure what will strike an editor's fancy. Over and again I've sent out ideas which I felt had practically no chance of being accepted, yet an editor said "yes." While you have to know your market and keep abreast of what editors are looking for, it never hurts to let your imagination soar a bit and hit them with occasional oddball ideas.   —*Robert Gaines*

If at First You Don't Succeed . .

A piece I wrote on palmistry hadn't sold at my first market selection, so I began sending it out to others and wound up with 38 refusals of it. This article was based on a book I had dug up at Brentano's at a cost of 50¢, written by Count someone, a Frenchman. I had sent for and received an okay from the ancient publishing firm to use some material from the book, though I didn't tell them I was joshing the whole bit.

After having sent the completed article to all the worthy markets I could think of, I started all over again and, as luck would have it, *Good Housekeeping* bought it the second time it reached them. It enjoyed quite a reader response.

Later on, *Cosmopolitan* suggested I prepare a compendium of all the semi-occult sciences; graphology, palmistry, phrenology and the like, supplied me with the books for research and paid a handsome fee.

The lesson in this is not to let a few rejections get you down if you feel your idea is good. In this case simple persistence ran a 50¢ investment up to $2,000.   —*William Lynch Vallèe*

Developing Your Automatic Idea Alert

The serious writer must constantly keep his senses alert for article ideas about him. He must train himself to look beyond the immediate surface interest of a minor incident, a regional event or a local personality. Encountering them he should ask himself, how might this little incident be expanded so as to have national ramification, could this regional event be the genesis of a countrywide trend, does this local person have a past life in which nearly anyone would be interested?

In gearing his mind to think continuously in this vein, the writer eventually finds the process becoming something of a second nature and he continues it ever more automatically, almost on a subconscious level. Then, when a good story possibility does appear—whether in newsprint, through word of mouth or in actual contact—the automatic mental relays click an alert and the writer's conscious attention zeroes in on the subject.

It's a great feeling when you've developed the knack to the point where something you encounter seems to rise up and shout, "I'm a great story—write me!"

Most good writers eventually develop this ability to some degree, but don't make the mistake of expecting it right away. It may take years of concerted effort on your part before the automatic alert system takes over.   —*Allan W. Eckert*

Chapter Two

FINDING AND USING SOURCES

Always Ask — The Answer is Often "Yes"

If over thirty years as a newspaper and magazine writer and interviewer has taught me one overriding lesson, it is this: be direct. This applies both in the writing and in the questioning of individuals for material. Looking back, I can pinpoint scores of stories which have been obtained or greatly strengthened because I went ahead and did something or asked questions which, at first thought, I tended to dismiss with "Oh, that's impossible" or "They certainly won't answer that question." Don't be afraid to ask for anything. At the worst, the answer can only be "No." You'd be surprised, though, how often the answer is "Yes." Let me give an example:

Some years ago I had an assignment from the *Reader's Digest* to do a world-wide roundup story on the activities of the Russian red trawlers. ("The Soviet's Little Known Wet War" was the title when it ran in the *RD*.) I had flown to St. John's, Newfoundland, rented a car and driven down to the U. S. Navy base at Argentia. From there I had flown aboard a Navy patrol plane which keeps tabs on these trawlers along the Grand Banks. The next morning, driving back to St. John's, I heard on the car radio that a large Russian oceanography ship, working with these trawlers on the Grand Banks, had put into St. John's the night before with an ill seaman. It was tied up at a local dock. My first inclination was that I wouldn't have a chance of getting aboard for a firsthand look and talks with the Russians.

I decided, "What do I have to lose by asking, though?"

In St. John's I turned in my rental car, loaded my bag into a taxi and told the driver to take me to the Russian ship in the dock area. It was a rainy, miserably cold Fall day. When we arrived at the pier I told the driver to wait. "This is only going to take me long enough to walk to the top of the gangplank and back down again," I said.

To the sailor on watch at the gangplank I explained I was a writer from the *Reader's Digest* and would like to talk to the Captain. "Yes sir," he replied in perfect English. It was as though I was expected. I was taken to a small office to wait. Within a few minutes the Captain appeared. He, too, spoke English. He couldn't have been more cordial. "Sure, anything you want to see," he told me. He took me to the chief scientist aboard. He, too, was cooperative. We toured the ship. If a door was locked and I asked what was behind it, the Captain would send a sailor for a key to unlock it. At every stop—and there were many—I had to have a drink of vodka, bottoms up! I'm glad to report that I upheld the integrity of American journalism by remaining on my feet all day.

Sure, I knew the Russians were feeding me a propaganda line. But I was also getting some very good material for my story—including the fact that when we inspected their photo lab aboard I saw reels of developed film taken of the St. John's Harbor when they'd steamed in the day before. The final result was that the material I gathered on this ship—merely by asking if I could come aboard—formed a large and important segment of the final, published article.   —*James H. Winchester*

You Can Get a Reader's Digest Index

Writers who subscribe to the *Reader's Digest* and keep the issues in their library for possible reference will be interested to learn that there is an "instant-research" *modus operandi* which will enable them to look up any previously published *Digest* article in jiffy time. The genie is an annual *Reader's Digest Index*. It's available, free, to all writers. You simply write the *Digest,* tell them you are a professional writer and ask to be put on their *Index* mailing list. They'll be glad to send you their *Index* at the end of every year. (And while you're at it, ask them to send you back Indexes for past years; they'll oblige until their supply is exhausted.)   *—Mort Weisinger*

Research Help from Radio "Hams"

Don't overlook the amateur radio system as a vehicle for communication in magazine article writing. Certainly the telephone is more reliable, more direct and more convenient but there are, or may be, occasions when ham radio can perform good service. Furthermore, you do not need to be a ham radio operator to take advantage of this service. Inquiry at various electronic distributors and examination of telephone listings will show the existence of several amateur radio clubs. The amateur radio operator is forbidden by FCC regulation to allow his facilities to be used for commercial purposes but in virtually all magazine writing there is no commercial aspect if the story has not been sold.

Many amateur radio operators (there are nearly 300,000 in the United States) have available equipment which can tie in their transmissions and receivings with the telephone system. This is called a phone patch. For example, suppose you wish to interview an engineer or physician at the South Pole. You might, through a local amateur radio society, find a near-by ham radio operator with experience in communication into Antarctica. Depending on ionospheric conditions he, in most cases, would be happy to arrange an interview with the man in Antarctica. It would not be necessary for you to go to his ham station; he would simply give you a ring when he made contact and hook you up to the transmission facilities in his shack. On two occasions I handled interviews in this manner— one with a physician in Antarctica and another an interview with ham radio operator Barry Goldwater.   *—Milton Golin*

Ideas and Research from Government Agency Reports

A matchless source of authentic and detailed information on government research projects and special programs, as well as the day-today operations of any particular executive agency of the government, is that specific agency's annual report to Congress. It is a thorough blueprint of the department's operations, findings, accomplishments, innovations and progress for the past year. Frequently, a careful scanning of the publication will suggest ideas for fresh magazine articles. Because it is addressed to Congress, whose members are presumably not all experts in the field of interest of the reporting agency, the text is usually not too complex for meaningful reading without recourse to technical encyclopedias.

Among agencies reporting are Defense, Agriculture, Interior, Treasury, State—in fact, each independent department of the executive branch. From the report of one such agency—the Atomic Energy Commission (before it was dismantled)—I received the initial impetus for two magazine articles, the first on atomic radiation preservation of foods, the second on use of atomic radiation as an extraordinary tool in crime detection.

Published each January, the reports are available from the Superintendent of Documents, United States Government Printing Office, Washington, D. C., 20402, or from the Office of Public Information of the specific agency.   —*Vernon Pizer*

More on Governmental Sources

The United States Government is the greatest research tool in the world, but only a few people know how to employ it adequately. Properly utilized, government sources can produce a wealth of information on almost any subject under the sun.

Most professional writers are aware of the obvious sources—the Library of Congress, the National Archives, the public information directors of government departments and bureaus. However, some sources of great value are less well known, among them these:

1. House Appropriations Hearings—Each year every governmental agency must appear before the Appropriations Committee to justify its budget. The volumes of testimony, which are printed

and released by the Committee, contain data on the operations of every department. Detailed justifications published in the volumes in fine print often contain clues to current and future operations which government agencies have not publicized (or will not).

For example, the agencies are required to report results of the programs previously undertaken—and sometimes these are unhappy results. Research on any agency or high government official should begin with the latest volume of appropriations testimony covering the proper department. It is available free of charge in person at the House Appropriations Committee, the Capitol. The Committee does not make a practice of filling mail requests, but a member of Congress can easily obtain the proper volume for you by mail, on request. Senate Appropriations hearings are somewhat less thorough, though occasionally useful.

2. Departmental Libraries—Nearly every government agency and bureau maintains a library of its own with specialized materials and, often, extensive clipping files of newspapers and magazines. Most librarians rarely see a magazine writer and enjoy helping. For the White House office, the library is the Bureau of the Budget library in the Executive Office Building.

3. Specialized Congressional Libraries—In addition to the Library of Congress, which maintains the nation's largest collection of books and the Legislative Reference Service, Congress maintains several other useful libraries. The Senate Library (Rooms 5 and 5A, Russell Bldg.) maintains a complete collection of Senate hearings, most House hearings, the *Congressional Record* and indexes and a useful clipping file.

The House Library (Room E-18, Cannon House Office Bldg.) contains similar material for the House of Representatives, though not so extensive or well organized.   —*Don Oberdorfer*

Seek Out Multiple Sources

I try hard to find the time to do all my own research. In the course of researching you turn up so many little things that make an article better—things you would never uncover if someone else did the research and simply gave you the bare facts. Here are some examples of what I mean:

A piece titled "Holland's Bulb Doctor" required me to investigate the scientific research behind tulips, daffodils and hyacinths. So my first step was to find an expert, Dr. Egbert van Slogteren. Before seeing him, I read extensively on the subject and learned as much as I could about Dr. van Slogteren.

Since my subject was a product exported from a foreign country to the United States, I talked to U. S. Department of Agriculture officials and to Netherlands customs officials. I asked them what they looked for before allowing bulbs to be shipped either out of Holland or into the United States. I approached this objectively, with no preconceived theories. This extra research not only gave me a good background on the subject and allowed me to be a more intelligent interviewer of the doctor, it also gave me a better "feel" for the subject than I would have had if I'd only contacted the doctor.

To do a good research job, one must be as thorough as possible and ready to acquire knowledge from several avenues if need be, rarely from only one. If you obtain material from but one or two sources, no matter how good, what is said is bound to be somewhat subjective, except where there is clearly one basic authority in a given subject or one company or association which is *the* information source.

Another time, for an article on congenital anomalies, I went to 12 hospitals and at each one an expert there told me about another expert at a different hospital, whom he thought I should see. Naturally, I followed up each lead. (Congenital anomalies, by the way, are the malformations with which babies are occasionally born.) Thus, in Philadelphia, I saw an expert on club feet and he told me about some wonderful work that was being done at the Boston Children's Hospital in congenital heart disease and I went to Boston.

At the Flower Fifth Avenue Hospital in New York, a doctor suggested that I go to Bellevue Hospital, also in Manhattan, to get some information about the research they were doing. It's like a spool of thread that unravels exciting information and provides you with a much better foundation for your finished article than a single source could possibly have done.

To take a third example, I did a piece for *True* about a man named Jake Sensibar, head of the Construction Aggregates Corporation. Mr. Sensibar was a charming but modest man. He cooperated by turning over his scrapbooks to me. Scrapbooks, if available, make excellent sources for fast information about your subject. The story that I was supposed to get from Mr. Sensibar was about his operation in draining swamps in Israel and his similar work on the Chicago lakefront.

However, talking only with Mr. Sensibar and studying his scrapbooks, I would never have learned what I did about him from the men who worked with him. I talked to these workmen and spoke to his associates. From them I got anecdotes giving me insights to this man which he, a quiet individual, would never have revealed.

The average interviewee tends to underrate himself. You must balance this by talking to others who are close to him. They may be business associates, members of his family, his secretary, his competitors or any "related" persons.   —*Amelia Lobsenz*

Some People Like Writing Letters

In the course of a year I sell about 20 magazine articles. During the same period I write about 2,000 business letters. The average is easy to calculate, but rather horrifying.

Half the letters are to editors, and I write rather than phone because, living in England, transatlantic phone calls are expensive. The rest are to various non-editors throughout the world and are mostly requests for information. Some of these people are public relations men whose job is looking after people like me. But a great many are men working hard in other occupations, who have no duty whatsoever to help writers. Through the years I have evolved an informal code of rules for getting the best out of all this paperwork.

1. If in doubt, always enclose a stamped, self-addressed envelope or postcard. Yes, it's a form of blackmail but, as is well known, blackmail pays handsomely.

2. "I wonder if you can help me?" seems a useful sort of phrase which evokes charitable feelings of grandeur in the most dyspeptic expert.

3. Give an idea how much you know already. This will save your expert from wasting time in repetition and will also impress him with your industry and seriousness. You've got to make him feel that he alone can supply your missing data.

4. Always write again your thanks for information, however stale, incomplete and irrelevant it may have been. You never know when the source may come up with something really hot. And for the occasional four-page letter which answers all your questions, provides a mass of unasked-for valuables and almost writes your article for you, don't hesitate to spend half an hour over a fulsome answer. "I wish everyone were as helpful as you."

5. Once initial contact is made, consider following up on the phone for further details. Some sources are at their best on paper, others orally. You can't tell. A tape recorder on the telephone is useful. However, if you use one, law as well as ethics obliges you to let your interviewee know he is being taped.

6. If you project a good anecdote to your source, he's sure to come back and cap it with two more. It's the oldest interviewing technique in the world—but writers somehow forget about it in their letters.

7. If your article quotes one of the sources, sometimes it will pay to let him see a draft (unless that is against the policy of your editor). Not only will he put you right on matters of detail, but also he will often add new material that had been lying dormant in his mind until some words of yours brought it out.

8. Ask for the editor's help in supplying important sources with copies of the article in print. After all, they deserve it. And from your own selfish point of view, remember that if you've made a good

job of it, your source will often come up with other ideas for your work, at least one in ten of which are usable.

9. When writing to a foreigner, write in English so that the meaning of your letter is totally unambiguous once he's got it translated. Unless his English is very good, invite him to reply in his own tongue for the same reason. He'll be much more fluent.

10. Never lose a source—and this is the most vital tip of the lot. My own 3 x 5 card index contains well over 1,000 names, all of whom I have dealt with in the past three years. They are cross-indexed under subjects. With a really fluent and intelligent source, make every effort to find out his other interests and fields of knowledge. A PR man whose job is in rubber, who gives bright and original information freely and who can be indexed as having expert knowledge of boar hunting in Poland, the Anzio beach, hotel management and hydraulics is worth his weight in gold. Send him, at least, a Christmas card. You never know when you're going to need him next.

—J. A. Maxtone Graham

Free Tearsheets from Magazines

Even experienced writers, I have learned much to my surprise, are unaware of the free research help—and tearsheets—they can get from some magazines. A letter to *Time,* for example, will get you a listing of all the articles run or mentions made by the magazine on a particular person or subject for the past one, two, five years or even longer. (Time-Life Building, Rockefeller Center, New York, N.Y. 10020.)

Similar information is also available from *Life Index* and *Fortune Index* about material published in their magazines. Each of these magazines will also mail you free tearsheets of any articles you want (however, generally not more than six at a time) if the issues are not too old. This saves the considerable cost involved in buying the complete back issues or in having the library make stats. Many other magazines will also furnish free tearsheets, although they may not furnish the bibliography the Time, Incorporated magazines do.

—Carl Bakal

Getting Information by Mail

The basic principle to remember is that the easier it is for someone to answer your query, the greater the likelihood that he will reply. When I write people for story information I almost always include a stamped, return-addressed envelope in which they can send me what I want. The return envelope, particularly one with a stamp on it, can be (I think) a big psychological incentive for getting your source to reply. Practically nobody likes to see a stamp go to waste. And the mere presence of an envelope addressed and ready for mailing overcomes another inertial roadblock.

It also helps if your source doesn't have to write you a letter with the information you want. I often suggest that he shouldn't bother taking time to write but "simply jot down your answers or comments at the bottom of this letter and return it to me in the enclosed envelope." I get a surprisingly high percentage of returns this way, usually via handwritten notes on the bottom of my letters. I'm sure that many letters would not be sent to me without my making it pretty easy to answer.

If I'm requesting a report, or material that will not fit in a return envelope but requires a package, I send instead an address sticker with my name and address on it, with stamps clipped to the sticker.

Obviously, return envelopes, stamps, etc. are not required with every query you send out. There are people, such as the PR men, who are eager for publicity, who will barrage you with material and information at the drop of a magazine name. (You may have to put up barricades to prevent being injured by the return.) —*Art Watkins*

Free Copies of Congressional Hearings

A few years ago I found out how to get a copy of a hot Congressional hearing when the first books containing the testimony roll off the government presses. I had dutifully written my congressmen and senators objecting to some of the provisions in the new Post Office Rate Bill back in '62. I also requested that my letter be made part of the hearing's record. This is the important point, since every person who testifies, either by mail or in person, is apparently entitled to a copy of the printed hearing. In due time, and after the hearings were completed and compiled in one of those green books, I got a copy of the hearing testimony in the mail. I got it quickly and along with all the other people who were first on the list to get copies of the testimony.

Now this gives you several advantages: One, you don't have to write the Government Printing Office for a copy—send whatever the charge may be, and then with limitless patience wait the usual several weeks for your copy; two, you don't have to write or press your congressman for a copy; and, three, you might otherwise forget all about the hearing and its testimony and not realize until months or even years later that the testimony has been published. (And then you'll generally find out about it when you read someone else's magazine article on the subject, with copious anecdotes and quotes culled from the hearing testimony.)   —*Art Watkins*

Utilizing Government Public Information Officers

Whatever medium you are aiming at, whatever the subject matter, chances are that somewhere in the vast labyrinth of the U. S. Government you will find some office—or perhaps just an officer— who can (a) assist you in the early or late stages of research; (b) direct you to related sources for additional information and material; (c) provide an authority who can be quoted, thus lending authentication to your magazine piece: (d) read the manuscript for accuracy, if desired.

There are few remaining U. S. Government agencies or sub-agencies which do not have a PR office. Almost invariably these offices maintain background morgues—clips, photos, biographies, anecdotes, etc.—which might be just the vein of gold for which you have been hunting. Not infrequently you will make the acquaintance of an Information Office (PIO man) who comes from a journalistic background like your own and who will not only aid you with depth material, but point out short cuts to people who count, information-wise, and feed you with story ideas in later assignments.

In my job as Director of Information for the Treasury Department's Bureau of Customs, I receive a steady stream of requests from freelance as well as staff writers all over the country, asking my help in a story on travel or anti-smuggling, import and tariff laws or what-have-you. Recently I helped a writer who wanted to know how many people arriving at JFK Airport in New York "try to get away with something" in the Customs area. I set up a conference-call interview with the Supervisory Inspector at the airport, and the writer (at no expense) was able to interview him for half an hour. A writer-photographer on *Life* did a piece on Customs after asking me to help by setting up a full schedule of interviews, providing a rich background file loaded with anecdotes, arranging for picture taking, etc.   —*Arthur Settel*

Sources on Military Stories

The men's adventure books are good markets for military adventure stories. However, all too few writers know that the New York Public Library has a bibliography of various World War I, World War II and Korean War unit histories. These are invaluable as source material on particular battles.

On the other hand, the service public information officers can provide the additional information about particular units which have alumni associations—information such as the executive secretary's name, address, and the like.

I found the name of the last man killed in World War II by looking for a divisional alumni association. Fortunately, this division had one and I got my story.   —*Edward Hymoff*

Subscribing to Readers' Guide

I subscribe to the *Readers' Guide to Periodical Literature* and keep a set at home. This investment ($62) is worth its weight in time saved in the library and in its easy accessibility when an idea strikes in the middle of the night. I find that the *Guide* has certain uses other than those for which it was designed. For example, apart from bibliographical work, it provides a quick and easy check on the spelling of names and, in some cases, on dates of birth. It can also give one a rough idea of when some important event occurred. Articles about the event may be dated weeks or months after the fact, but the *Guide* helps you to zero in.

Its chief use, however, is in locating the dates of previously published articles. Since I also maintain my own files of *Time, Newsweek, Fortune, Business Week, Harper's* and other magazines, the *Guide* permits me to do a lot of preliminary research right in my own room, rather than at the library.   —*Alvin Toffler*

Use the Public Relations Man's Services

When researching, particularly in the fields of business and industry, don't fail to contact the public relations man for the firm or individual you're planning to write about. Bear in mind that his job was created to fill your needs.

The experienced public relations man almost always has on file a biography he has prepared on his client and a fact sheet about the company. Copies of these will be sent to you immediately upon request. In addition, the PR man worth his salt will help arrange interviews for you and prepare special materials, including anecdotes.

The dedicated PR man will even go so far as to do a great deal of research for you in libraries and elsewhere. In effect, he will quite often become a valuable right hand in getting you off to a good start on the story you're preparing.

Since I am *both* a writer and the head of a New York based public relations firm—with many national clients—and lecture extensively on the subject, I feel qualified to say that the public relations person's duty to his client is to supply any needed outlines, research or even rough drafts. These rough drafts can serve as the basis for fine articles for national magazines.

Finally, the good public relations person will give you a "fact check" when you have finished writing your piece. He will even present the material to his client to make sure that it is absolutely correct. This is a most valuable service to all concerned.

An experienced public relations man, knowing that a client becomes an interesting magazine subject only if he is shown as a fullbodied, many-faceted personality, will give you a frank description of his client. This does not mean that the writer will not want to meet the "personality" or company executives first hand. In fact, to get the best article he should, and the public relations man will set up such interviews for the writer. —*Amelia Lobsenz*

Buy Back-Date Magazines to Save Research Time

I save a lot of time by making use of back issue magazine dealers. When I have completed a bibliography, instead of going to the library to copy out what I need, I simply telephone a dealer in backdate magazines and order the items I need. That same day I can pick them up, return to my office and pluck what I need out of them. This saves me hours of copying and has contributed considerably to reducing the size of the writing callous on my right middle finger.

Incidentally, I found after a while that different back-issue companies specialize in different kinds of publications. There are even a few—mainly used by libraries—that carry a wide range of scholarly journals. Buying up back-date magazines helps me get the material on my bibliography quickly and spares me hours of sitting in a library. The cost of these back issues is by no means exorbitant and, at least as I see it, well worth every nickel. —*Alvin Toffler*

More on Back-Date Magazines

Note-taking is too time consuming not to avoid when possible. When I was doing a piece on Thomas Edison for *Reader's Digest,* I was told by Edison's son of a long piece on his father that had run in *Harper's* in 1932. I checked *Reader's Guide,* got the exact date, then went to the ABC Magazine Shop in Chicago and got my issue for a dollar or two—and saved five or ten dollars worth of note-taking time in the library, plus having the article for my permanent file. Photo copies made on machines available in most large libraries serve somewhat the some purpose.   *—Alfred Balk*

For Business Research, Play the Market

Thanks to Securities and Exchange Commission and Stock Exchange regulations, more information is available on companies than writers who do not regularly handle business subjects realize. Before any company can sell stock to the public, it is required to file an extremely detailed prospectus, giving its history, past sales and profits or losses, biographies of executives, prospects, and the like. The salaries of the three highest paid officers of any listed company are public information. By consulting the proxy statements at the New York Stock Exchange you can find the amount of stock in the company owned by any officer or director. They are required by law to report any buying or selling of it. If you need still more information, you can buy stock in any company that has it for sale and ask questions as a part owner of the business. I did this with Tiffany & Co., obtained information for a magazine article and a book chapter at two stockholders' meetings and, when a struggle for control developed, sold my 10 shares at a profit of $300.   *—Tom Mahoney*

For Accuracy, Check Your Information Firsthand

I do not believe in secondhand research. I refuse to rely on the so-called "basic" research that involves copying and repeating previously published information, statistics or what-have-you. I believe in going to the horse's mouth to secure up-to-date information from some responsible individual, group or agency concerned with the subject. And if the information doesn't seem to make me "comfortable"— if there are any nagging doubts (and there often are!)—I'll just keep checking out until I'm satisfied.

Doing a documentary on jailing of mental patients, for example, I received reports from officials in various parts of the country that state or county laws and statutes specifically prohibited holding mental cases in jail. Knowing full well that laws are frequently honored more in breach than in observance and suspicious that some of the officials merely quoted the law with no further comment, I did some firsthand unannounced visiting to check up.

In one Florida county, I found that while the law said no mental cases were ever to be jailed, the county hospital refused to take them in for observation and examination. So, let's say your wife or grandpa is acting queer or hallucinating. You call the cops. "Unofficially" they tell you—look, just take the person and put him out on the sidewalk in front of your house. We'll then pick him up for "vagrancy" or "public drunkenness." We'll take him to jail. Then, we'll call up the hospital and tell them we've got a mentally disturbed *prisoner*. Because we hold (in jail) some of the patients they can't handle, they reciprocate on our prisoners.

Another example: While doing a documentary on jailing of children, I learned there is a state law in Minnesota prohibiting holding juveniles in jail. The law is categoric. So what happened when I checked it out in Minneapolis? Almost 2,000 kids were held in jail for varying periods in 1962. Aside from the reasons police and authorities gave for this prohibited practice, the cops "interpreted" the law as applying only to kids who had already had a hearing in juvenile court. Up to that point, police said, the law did not apply. So the kids stayed (and still stay) in jail.

I can't stress too much the importance of firsthand checking. I appreciate the fact that sometimes this might be prohibitive in terms of time and money. On the other hand, when you're dealing with an important or controversial subject you just can't take chances—you can ruin the whole piece with a few glaring inaccuracies. —*Sid Ross*

How to Make Contacts in Strange Cities

One of the problems in researching certain types of articles in strange cities is establishing rapport with the local business community. In other words, how do you uncover people with something pertinent to say? One way I dig up leads is by showing up at the local Kiwanis meeting (there's usually one every week), introducing myself and sitting down. Kiwanians are generally very gregarious people and soon you can have them talking about what you want to hear. Good quotes result and they often suggest other people to see. I do this since I used to work on the staff of *The Kiwanis Magazine* and still contribute articles to it. But any writer could drop in on a meeting, give a reasonable excuse for his being there and sit in. This would probably work with Lions and Rotary, too. Sometimes I get the club secretary's name and call him in advance. If you are not a member of the service club you'd like to visit, be certain first to contact one of the club's officers, explain your position and ask permission to attend.

—Hal Higdon

Free PR Service Assists with Research

My wife, Betty, has developed a short-cut for freelance writers seeking specific information, enabling them to reach hundreds of public relations people at one time. She runs a newsletter called Party Line, which is subscribed to by PR men across the country and in all aspects of public relations: commercial, nonprofit, etc. Where you have a specific request, drop a note to Mrs. Betty Yarmon, 165 East 66th Street, N.Y., N.Y., 10021. If you want to hide the theme of your article or the magazine for which it is being prepared, by all means do so, so long as your request is worded specifically enough so that the PR sources can catch at a glance just what it is you want from them. List a deadline if you wish.

I know this works. Friends of mine in the freelance business repeatedly tell me that an item in Party Line has helped them in researching a piece in a fraction of the time it would have taken them to call up a dozen sources—assuming they could have found out who had the pertinent information for them. The newsletter comes out each Monday. Mrs. Yarmon will be glad to send you a current issue; it can give you an idea of the way items asking for information are phrased. Book-writers are invited to take advantage of this, too.

Such a listing is absolutely free, no strings. The subscribers pay the freight.   —*Morton Yarmon*

Get Your Friends Into the Act

Sometimes friends or relatives can turn out to be excellent sources for research material. Recently I was having a hard time finding background data for an article on "The New Math." I mentioned this at the table during a dinner party. Within a week I was swamped with pamphlets, books and reference sources. Most of the "researchers" seemed genuinely flattered at being able to contribute to a "major article."   —*S. L. Englebardt*

Making the Most of Associations

In dealing with organizations—trade, professional, religious, scientific or whatever—headquarters of the national body may best be counted upon for comments concerning the group's policies and for country-wide statistics. However, for human interest material, member chapters at the state or local level are more apt to be of help to you.

One of the best ways to locate the right organizational sources for a particular article is to study your telephone book. Then check over the Manhattan section of the New York City phone directory— or possibly the directories for Washington, D.C., Chicago or Los Angeles. These can lead you to groups pertinent to your project *if* you remember a few key words. See what useful leads turn up when you look under headings beginning:

National . . .
National Association of . . .
International . . .
Society . . .
Brotherhood . . .

. . . as well as others of this ilk. The name of your subject, be it retail or psychological, may be followed in the directories by the full name of a society that could be helpful to you.

In some places you'll find that the classified pages carry a section worthwhile consulting, called "Organizations." Also, any local branch of a national organization will be glad to provide you with the address of its national headquarters.

From time to time, compendiums of organizations are published. Obviously, some of the information is outdated before publication date, since new officers are elected annually in many of these groups. However, local chapters should be able to tell you who the current national officers are. National headquarters locations do not often change.

Some fields boast a greater number of national bodies than others, but each group will usually be covering a specifically defined area. Just what that is may be described in a directory, although in some cases you may have to write for fuller details.

It is not uncommon in the preparation of an article to contact several—even many—different organizations to get all the information you need. For instance, when I was preparing the article "Buckle Up for a Safe Flight" for *Today's Health,* I had contact with the Civil Aeronautics Board, Department of Commerce and the Federal Aviation Agency in Washington, as well as writing to, calling or holding personal interviews with officers of Flight Safety Foundation, Air Transport Association, Air Traffic Control Association, Inc., Flying Physicians Association, Air Line Dispatcher's Association International, the Ninety-Nines, Inc., and the Air Line Pilots Association.   *—Beatrice Schapper*

Chapter Three

WORKING IN LIBRARIES

You Can Get Any Book through Interlibrary Loan

Any number of books impossible to find in your city can be yours to consult for a few cents each, if you have access to a library that cooperates with others in the interlibrary loan system. First step is to determine which library has the book you are seeking. Next step is to apply through your local library for the out-of-town library to lend the book to it, for your use. Usually the fee charged for this interlibrary loan service is limited to the postage plus insurance. When the book arrives at your local library, you must read it there so that it remains under the library's surveillance.

The New York Public Library does not take part in this program, but many others in New York do. The Library of Congress in Washington, D. C., biggest of them all, does cooperate and, in one fiscal year it circulated more than 35,000 volumes to 2,100 borrowing libraries outside the Washington area. A quick way to determine whether the Library of Congress has the particular book you want is to write to your own Congressman and ask him to find out for you.   *—Alden Todd*

Seek Out Books on Your Subject

We all know that the *Readers' Guide to Periodical Literature* is an excellent source for bibliographical material, but it is an obvious source. All writers go there. And if they find that the subject is not listed there, or is sparsely covered, quite frequently they will give up.

What some writers don't do is go one step further. For example, I was doing a piece on Tiffany's for *Reader's Digest*. But Tiffany's did not want to cooperate and refused to grant an interview. Every writer who had previously tried to profile Tiffany's in print had met with the same resistance. When they looked up Tiffany's in the *Readers' Guide* they found little that could be used.

It occurred to me to go to the card file of books in the Public Library and, sure enough, back around 1900 one of Tiffany's officers had written an entire book on this fabulous jewelry store. It was a veritable Klondike of information, enough to serve as the backbone for my eventual article, where I quoted liberally. It was all there, waiting to be mined, and no writer had thought of looking it up. So never stop with the *Readers' Guide;* go on and see what you can find under "books."   *—Mort Weisinger*

Getting Factual Information by Phone from Libraries

Many libraries will give you standard reference information over the phone. Some librarians, I've found, consider it a challenge to be asked hard questions. They will go to extraordinary lengths to find the answer. If I need to know the circulation of a newspaper or magazine, for example, or any statistic which I can't find in the *World Almanac,* I call the reference desk of the library.

Once, for an historical piece, I wanted to know how long it took a traveler to go from Philadelphia to New York in 1735. "Call me back in twenty minutes," the reference librarian said. When I called back he gave me the length of time (three to four days), the routes and points where travelers switched from stagecoach to ferry boat. It would have cost me two hours or more to go to the library to look up this information on my own—and that's longer than it takes to go from Philadelphia to New York today.   *—Marvin Weisbord*

Recording Notes in the Library

Normally, when I go to the library I just take out a notebook and scribble what I need into it. But if I am going to cover a lot of material I use a tape recorder. That way I can operate faster and cut my library time in half. Most libraries have corners or places in the stacks where the librarians will allow you to use a tape recorder if you ask politely in advance.   —*Hal Higdon*

Where to Find It in the Library

An alert, helpful and well-trained reference librarian is the best possible source of information on where and how to find what you want in library reference books. But if such a person is not available, the next best friend of the research worker is the soft-cover booklet, *Reference Books,* published by Enoch Pratt Free Library of Baltimore, Maryland. No other brief guide for students and library users approaches it for quality.

The contents of the 135-page booklet are indexed by type of book, subject, author and editor. A descriptive paragraph tells what is contained in each of the reference books most likely to be found in American libraries. The Enoch Pratt Free Library (at 400 Cathedral Street, Baltimore, MD 21201) will mail the latest edition of *Reference Books* (1978) upon payment of $2.50, and it is worth every cent in time saved and research completed.   —*Alden Todd*

Personal Digging in Libraries Pays Off

Most writers (myself especially) don't, I think, use public libraries enough. The library profession is full of devoted persons trying to be useful and, as a rule, always pleased when they can be of help. Small town librarians (professionals) are especially helpful and what they don't have they'll get from the county seat, a library center or the Library of Congress, if necessary. To know your way around a library is an asset. Public libraries are gold mines. Sometimes it takes digging to get the metal out, but it is pure gold when it comes.
                                                        —*John R. Tunis*

Using the Times Index for Anecdote Leads

If you are desperate for anecdotes, search for some through the *New York Times Index.* Break your subject down to as many lead words as possible. They may lead you, through the *Index,* to colorful stories from the news. They may also enlarge your research trove and make you feel you have to rewrite your article; but this is the cross perfectionists must bear. Of course, access to a newspaper morgue would be a better source of colorful material, but too few of us have that advantage.   *—José Schorr*

Using a Researcher for Preliminary Work

I hate working in libraries. I find them impersonal and intimidating; and you waste so much time going to and fro and hunting for books when you're there. So, as much as possible, I hire a researcher to check *Readers' Guide* and the card catalog. Then I either ask the researcher to borrow and bring me the books I need with pertinent pages marked with paper clips or I have her buy the books and bring them to me all set up likewise. Sometimes I may have the researcher actually give the book a preliminary reading and write up a concise report for me on its contents and approach. With magazines, I belong to a private library that lets most of them circulate, so the researcher brings me the issues with pieces that seem to tie in with the one I'm working on or, if the magazine does not circulate, I have it photostatted. If the library doesn't have it, the researcher buys a back-copy at one of the Sixth Avenue shops. If I pay a researcher up to $10 an hour for this sort of thing, I'm still ahead because my time is worth more than that.   *—Gerald Walker*

Reading the Footnotes

"When you've heard six eyewitnesses describe an accident," goes an old reporter's axiom, "you begin to wonder about history." You wonder even more when you read, for example, diary entries by any six men who attended the same meeting of the President's Cabinet.

For this reason it's essential, especially in historical work, to read the footnotes. Who said it? Why? When? Where did *he* get it? These elements of good reporting apply as much to past events as to this morning's news. In any piece of prolonged research you soon recognize the reliable sources. You learn which footnotes to trust and which to doubt. When you see an alleged fact that conflicts with what you know, you can go to the original and check it out. Sometimes you can trace a "fact" back through three or four sources, all of whom cribbed it from the same man. And he made it up.

I once did a profile of Richard K. Fox, who edited the *Police Gazette* around the turn of the century. *The Dictionary of American Biography* gave Fox two marriages. Checking the DAB's sources, I found one to be an inaccurate magazine article copied largely from another inaccurate article written 20 years before. Fox had been married three times. (His second wife, the omitted one, was by far the most interesting. She ran off with a younger man, taking the family silver.) The first magazine article also gave a birthdate for Fox which, as near as I can tell, the writer invented. Fox himself, writing in the *Police Gazette,* gave a different date. You can multiply these examples endlessly—if you check the footnotes.

—*Marvin Weisbord*

Flagging Information in Books

When flagging information in a book, I use different size and differently colored bookmarks to denote various sub-topics (good quotes, dates, anecdotes, etc.) and write on the bookmarks what each one flags. —*Alfred Balk*

Chapter Four

USING THE TELEPHONE

Planning Helps Telephone Interviews

Time is money where long-distance telephone interviews are concerned. I make it a point to be methodical when doing such interviews.

First of all, I keep beside me a sheet of paper on which I've jotted down information on the person I'm interviewing. Also, I've put down the names of others he knows and to whom he or I might refer during our conversation.

I recall an assignment that required in-depth reporting on a prominent medical personality. But he was a reluctant individual. I had to go to others who knew him in his distant past. Since they were scattered throughout the nation, much of this interviewing had to be confined to the telephone. Careful dossiers on each helped me to win their confidence (for prominent persons are invariably pleased when others know something of the particulars that led to their success) and further helped me to pinpoint persons and events that aided my interviewees in recalling specific situations that made for interesting anecdotes. My dossiers were a kind of cross-reference on each other. All the pieces fitted together like a jigsaw puzzle and it was rarely necessary to call anyone back.

Secondly, I keep before me a carefully planned list of questions designed to help me pin down the interview to its essentials in the briefest possible time. This is not simply a money-saving gesture but an organizational technique which recognizes that the interviewee's time may be limited. I number each question and relate the answers to these numbers. This saves the trouble of writing down material already implicit in the question's topic and further allows me to relate subsequent answers to previous questions when necessary. Tape recording a telephone interview, of course, eliminates this bother, but I prefer the written notes. They enable me to jot down impressions as the conversation proceeds.

Aside from the personal dossier and question list, I make sure to read back quotable material then and there and ask for permission to quote. Whenever possible, I also try to get permission to refine a quote if need be. Of course, in cases where quotable material is controversial, I make it a point to get written confirmation or go on record by dropping a short note to the interviewee after the call.

—*Arthur Henley*

Using the Phone to Give a Piece Nationwide Scope

While a face-to-face session is generally far more productive, the phone interview has some special virtues. It can have a sense of urgency. On a long-distance call, your source is apt to feel impelled to open up because you've bothered to call him all the way from your city to his. You probably catch him off guard. He talks more freely because he doesn't see you taking notes. Talking through an impersonal telephone to a faceless interviewer, he's not likely to feel self-conscious and hold back.

The phone interview also can be time-saving and money-saving. I've found it most effective in the roundup, where bits and pieces have to be gathered from scattered sources.

On one recent story, I had to interview as many pilots as possible who had been wounded in a current fracas overseas. I was lucky to catch one major in New York, where he had come on a one-day visit. He gave me the name of another veteran who was being patched up in Walter Reed Hospital in Washington. Since I had a tight deadline, I couldn't spare the day in Washington, so I conducted an hour-long phone interview with the man at Walter Reed. In the bed next to him was another pilot. I interviewed him, too, and picked up the name and address of a third pilot in Alabama. It worked like a chain reaction. In all, I talked by phone to eight men. If I had hopped around by plane, it would have taken me at least a week to get my story and I'd have missed my deadline.

Another example involved a medical piece I worked up for a weekly. After personal interviews with several medical authorities, I had a list of 50 special clinics involved in my story. I selected a half-dozen scattered throughout the country to give my piece nationwide scope.

First I wrote a short letter to the medical director at each of the clinics. I included three or four key questions and indicated I'd phone for the answers on a specific date. This gave my sources time to gather statistics, a statement of evaluation and the like. When I did phone, my medical directors were ready for me and I could ask them further questions based on their answers. The roundup story must have read as if I'd been traveling about the country.

The phone interview is useful, too, when you want a short quote from an expert. It's easier, of course, if you've used the authority in some previous story and you don't have to go through the business of introducing yourself.

To get the most out of a tough source, when feasible I try to put my phone calls through during an evening, when my target is away from his office and presumably more relaxed after a drink and a meal—and therefore more cooperative and voluble. Catch him at his office and you might get a brush-off.

Sometimes a phone call brings unexpectedly happy results. Once, on a story for a distaff magazine, I was stuck for a few important details. The only person who had these facts was an oilman in Oklahoma City. The few facts I needed didn't warrant the trip, so naturally I telephoned him. It turned out he had a lot more information than I suspected. I expressed delight and enthusiasm, the enthusiasm became infectious and two days later my oilman flew to New York for an interview with me that lasted an entire afternoon.

—Theodore Irwin

Calls from a Pay Phone Can't be Ignored

Do you have trouble bearding VIP lions in their dens for quotes? Soliciting celebs via the mails is hazardous; a secretary will reply with a form polite refusal; often your letter will lie in limbo and never be acknowledged. During the past several years I have developed a sure-fire gimmick which works nine out of ten times. I simply ensconce myself in a public telephone booth and fortify myself with a stack of quarters and dimes. Then I phone the celebrity at his office, person-to-person. When I reach him, the operator invariably says: "I have your party. Please deposit $3.25." Then I go into my ritual of inserting 13 quarters.

Can you imagine the reaction of the subject at the other end? When I identify myself as a freelance writer, he knows I have invested $3.25 of my own hard-earned money (not a big magazine's!) and he immediately feels obligated. If I had phoned him from my home phone, he might curtly tell me he's busy and to send him a letter. But when he knows I've shelled out hard cash, a fact which has registered on him via the tolling of the coins, he is sympathetic, helpful and most cooperative. He regards me as an underdog and becomes quite loquacious. (Once when I phoned Senator Robert Kennedy and my time ran out, he told the operator to charge him for the extra minutes.)

Should you decide to experiment with this technique, make it a point to phone your subject during the lunch hour. Usually, his secretaries will be out for their lunch. I have found that most famous folk, particularly women, are so busy they usually send out for their lunch and eat at their desk. Consequently, they will answer the phone themselves when you call. But be careful to check on the time zone difference!   —*Mort Weisinger*

Other Help from the Telephone Company

You can get free telephone directories for many areas near where you live by dialing the local telephone business office and asking for them. You can also get classified directories but they cost money and also the directories for distant cities that you frequently must call, such as Washington, D.C.; these will cost you a dollar or two. It can be well worth it if you have frequent use for these directories.

—*Art Watkins*

Take Advantage of Low Night Phone Rates

For certain kinds of research the long-distance telephone call is fastest, best and most economical. Many people are too busy to answer letters, but few can resist a long-distance call. In the evening you can call station-to-station for little more than $1 for the first three minutes anywhere in continental U.S.   —*Tom Mahoney*

Using the Phone for Hard-to-Reach Interviewees

Long-distance calls are a widely underrated research tool. You can get some people by phone who won't see you if you're in their city. I don't hesitate to phone people for a quote or other material and I find it useful, for lengthy phone interviews, to send suggested questions ahead to give them time to collect their material and their thoughts.

When I was working with Thomas Edison's son, Charles, former governor of New Jersey who now lives in New York City, on an Unforgettable Character story for *Reader's Digest,* I needed two interviews of some length. He gave me one in New York. I returned home. Then, instead of my returning, he asked that we finish by phone. We did—a 40-minute long-distance conversation that gave me everything else that I needed.

Another time, when working on a story about Irving Berlin, I couldn't get an early appointment with him at his office, but he gladly spent a half hour chatting with me by phone.   —*Alfred Balk*

Saving Money with Station-to-Station Calls

I sometimes make station-to-station phone calls to sources in distant cities, rather than the usual person-to-person calls which cost more. I draw the line here at those people or sources who will unquestionably want to talk with me and call me back at their expense, if necessary, because such people are so highly interested in contributing to the article I'm writing or because they know me from previous articles. It's therefore much cheaper to talk to them at station-to-station charges, rather than at person-to-person rates. Roughly half the time I catch my quarry at his desk and he answers the phone. If he's not in, I simply talk to his secretary or wife or PR man, state my business in such a way that the source will call me back, often at his firm's expense, just as soon as he returns to his office (or so I like to think).   —*Art Watkins*

Setting Up the Tape Recorded Phone Interview

I do a lot of my work with a tape recorder. Many of my magazine interviews are tape recorded telephone conversations and I find that subjects are most cooperative if they are handled right.

For example, set the subject at ease by informing him that you want the interview one or two days after the first telephone contact. Specifically, that you want to give him a day or two to recollect an incident or compose his thoughts. Then you should set up a time to phone. Because long-distance telephone rates drop tremendously in the evening, you might try to set up the call for such a time.

Now, once you've told the subject that you want to talk with him again following the initial contact, he's usually amenable to talking right then and there. If he opens up, and only the interviewer can tell by the way the conversation is going, then ask his permission to record the conversation. If he seems reluctant but wants to have time to recall incidents and go through personal papers to refresh his memory, undoubtedly you'll discover that during the initial conversation he has given you enough interesting facts off the top of his head, so to speak, that from them you can base the questions to follow during the next formal, recorded interview.

I find that the use of a tape recorder gives me unusual accuracy and permits me to concentrate on the questions and the interview instead of concentrating on writing down answers and losing a train of thought. Moreover, the tape recorder doesn't waste time, while writing down answers does.

I use the services of a typist to transcribe my taped interviews. I find that the typed transcript can be scissored so that the various categories of the subject can be put in proper place in the outline of the article. *—Edward Hymoff*

Chapter Five

INTERVIEWING

Interview for Opinions, not Facts

When interviewing provocative people—who are usually expert in the field in which you are writing at the moment—it's a terrible waste of what is probably a limited amount of interview time to use that time getting facts or background that could be obtained elsewhere. The tone of an interview can frequently be set by the first question. If it is banal, the whole interview may collapse; if it is thoughtful and provocative, the subject may be stimulated into quotations that will make the story.

The writer should be interested primarily in the *opinions* and *philosophy* of the people he is interviewing. Asking Neil Simon what was his first play is not evocative; you can find this out from his press agent. But asking him what play he considers his best is evocative—because it solicits an opinion only he can provide. Facts should be primary in an interview only when the writer is on a news story, talking with a source that has access to facts not available elsewhere. However, quotable opinion or philosophy can only be sparked by intelligent questions and they, in turn, can only be asked when the reporter has prepared himself ahead of time. There is no excuse for a magazine writer, working at a much more leisurely pace than a newspaper reporter, not to background himself in this way before an interview.

Before an interview with Rex Harrison, I read as much as I could find about him and went in well-heeled with information.

Among other things, I learned he had known George Bernard Shaw, had worked in several of his plays where Shaw took a direct hand in the production and had great respect for him. I was ushered in to meet Harrison under rather trying conditions. He had just finished filming "My Fair Lady" and was involved in the turmoil of farewells, packing and other distractions. Circumstances seemed less than ideal for an interview. Happily, however, the first question I asked him was: "Do you think Shaw would have approved of the ending of 'My Fair Lady?' " The question intrigued him and he sat down and pondered it, then answered at some length. From that time on Harrison was relaxed, easy, affable—and spouting aphorisms. On the way out the press agent exhaled audibly. "I was worried," he said. "I took a radio interviewer in there yesterday to tape a show and his questions were so banal that Harrison got irritated and just answered them 'yes' or 'no.' The whole thing turned into a shambles."

Backgrounding is even more urgent on a story involving some technical areas. For example, I did a lengthy piece on the seven Mercury Astronauts (that later turned into a book) early in the manned space program. My interview time with them had to be caught on the run, in fits and starts, between a lot of frenetic activity. There was simply no time for leisurely conversation building up to fresh and quotable material. In this instance I spent several weeks studying the technical aspects of the space program so I could ask meaningful questions when and if I was able to corner the Astronauts for interviews.   —*Joseph N. Bell*

The Marathon Interview: Catch Your Man at Leisure

Before interviewing a busy and important man who may be full of the information I need, I try to save his time, especially if he is to be the subject of my article and hence must consent to hours of questioning. First I read up on him and his field and interview all lesser people on my list. I let him know I've done this so he realizes I won't waste his time with questions someone else can answer. Then, in negotiating for the key interview with him, I suggest we plan it for a

time when he can talk while doing something else—driving somewhere or fishing or washing his car. If this is impossible, I suggest
mealtime or a drink after work. (The office is the worst of all
settings for a major interview, I find.)

During extended informal interviews of this kind, there can be
long lulls or digressions without any feeling of awkwardness. Lulls
give me time to digest what he's said and think up new questions. A
relaxed atmosphere and freedom from interruptions encourage him
to ramble and reminisce more than he'd be likely to in a formal
interview across a desk; and often the rambling uncovers surprisingly
valuable bits of fact or color. I get the best material when I manage
to accompany an interviewee on a long trip; next best when I'm
lounging with him in the sun or sitting around at his home. The basic
strategy, of course, is to get several informal hours with him, yet not
cut into his work or recreation.   —*Keith Monroe*

A Note from Your Magazine Helps Arrange Interviews

As a time-saver in arranging interviews, particularly sticky ones, I
ask the magazine to send me a one sentence note on their letterhead
saying simply that they are assigning me to the story. I photocopy
this note and send it with my own letter requesting interviews. This
invariably saves a great deal of explaining and usually gets immediate
results.   —*Joseph N. Bell*

The Gang Interview

When seeking anecdotes and color, I find that talking with several
people together seems more productive than interviewing each singly,
especially if they feel at ease with each other. Chatting over drinks
or a leisurely meal, they remind one another of interesting information and sometimes get into disagreements that stimulate them to
unexpected revelations. You save time you would otherwise spend
putting the same questions to each of the sources individually. You
also simplify your job of checking for accuracy; if all these sources
confirm what one of them says, further verification of it is often
unnecessary.   —*Keith Monroe*

Edit While He Talks

I do my editing while interviewing and I find it saves me many laborious hours of transcribing inanities and then weeding them out when I get around to writing my story. That's why I don't use a tape recorder—unless the interview is so controversial or antagonistic that I will need proof of quotations after publication. Normally I make notes during interviews only of the statements that I feel are are of value and pertinent to my story. Thus repetitions, non-responses and small talk don't get into my notes and thus don't get in the way when I'm organizing my material to write. Admittedly, I may miss a few things this way, but the time and effort saved more than makes up for this risk.   —*Joseph N. Bell*

For Depth Interviews, Go Back Several Times

Writing the so-called "as-told-to" pieces is a skill unto itself, especially if it involves your subject remembering events that occurred months or years before. I find that several short interviews with the subject are more satisfactory than one long one. During the first interview I try to cover everything. Then at later interviews I say, "Let's go over this one incident in detail," but after going over the incident I go over everything else, too. At subsequent interviews I keep running over old ground, listening patiently to the stories and anecdotes I've heard told the same way many times before. I find that each time the subject usually remembers some little thing he forgot to tell me the first time. It helps, if your deadline permits, to space the interviews a week or so apart. I've found that you can get 95 per cent of the information you want in your first interview, but the 5 per cent that you have to bleed for is often the difference between a good article and a merely acceptable one.   —*Hal Higdon*

Getting More than "The Image"

To get the provocative opinion, the revealing quote, the recital of first person experience, the writer must be analyst, private eye, soothing fan, prosecuting attorney. He has to gain his subject's confidence but not be taken in by cliche answers. Nor should he approach an interview with cliche questions or expectations. The writer may find a minister, for example, who approves of pre-marital sex but if he assumes at the outset that this is improbable, he'll never ask the right questions and never get the story.

The objective is to have a free and easy conversation so that you can find out what the other person is really like. Sometimes it can be difficult because many authorities and celebrities have developed conversational reflexes to protect themselves from professional probers. The man on the street, or the housewife in the kitchen, is more spontaneous. They will tell all because nobody has ever bothered to ask them before. By contrast, the public interviewee is a wary beast and must be stalked cautiously. Here are some devices I find useful in breaking down the public relations facade.

Begin by letting him tell you the story he wants to see in print. If he is involved in a research project, ask him how he happened to think of it, how much work is involved, what results are anticipated. This is the warmup. He is persuaded that you are interested in him and wish only to publicize his efforts. (You may indeed do precisely that.) Additionally, however, you need to discover what is really going on, how it fits into other efforts, how genuine are his claims. You have to establish the "truth," not only what he is determined to tell you.

While he talks you should be framing questions to check out the inconsistent or self-serving parts of the recital. You are then prepared to ask such questions as, "Hasn't something of this kind been done before?" or "How do you justify the expense when the results are inconclusive?" You want to show him that you are, at least, skeptical; that you are not taken in by the "gee whiz" public relations image. Hopefully, he will rise to the bait. If he becomes a bit angry you can catch him off guard. He will probably say more than he intended to. And you will get some real live quotes, not just the predictable institutionalized handout.

Use your pencil as a prod when the interview bogs down. Put it down with an air of "I guess you're not ready to tell me any more," and you can usually stimulate him to talk. If he feels you are bored he may make an effort to give.

If you sense he is telling you something off the record (although he doesn't insist that it be that) don't write it down. You'll scare him. Try to remember it though and, later when he's droning on about statistics or material easily available to you, get the goodie on paper.

The more authentic the quote, the better. Don't paraphrase it. Not only will you get into trouble later when he complains, "I never said that," but you weaken the story. People express themselves in very personal language. Try to capture it verbatim.

Finally, pray that your subject will not ask to see the piece before publication. If he does, tell him you will check any direct quotes with him for accuracy but don't show him the whole story. Extract his comments and send them along. Invariably people want to rewrite their own statements to make them sound less original, less human.

Close your notebook, signaling that the ordeal is at an end—but don't close your ears. You may get the most revealing story just as you go out the door. (People generally break down when they think they're safe.) Don't wait until you get home to write it down. Do it as soon as you're out of earshot.   —*Mary Anne Guitar*

Getting Your Best Quotes Off the Cuff

If the interviewee is important to the story and has time, do not rush the interview. My practice is this: at some point I stop asking formal questions, close my notebook and pocket the pen, indicating the interview is over and now we're just two people chatting. The other person relaxes. I don't. We talk for another 20 minutes or so. In this period I often obtain the best material because the interviewee is more at ease and more spontaneous.

For example, I had interviewed the doctor of a boy who nearly died after being severely burned in an accident. I was leaving her

office and casually tossed off some comment about the importance
of courage in burn cases.

"Yes," she said, "Bobby will make it. He's proud of his life."
That quote became my ending.   —*Joseph P. Blank*

To See a Celebrity, Ask His Friends

Writing to a celebrity to request an interview can be a very one-sided
correspondence. Letters—even wires—are often ignored or inter-
cepted by an insecure press agent who wants you to interview him.
First try the publicity man, but if he doesn't comply—and if you have
a legitimate assignment and not just a desire to meet the personality
—ignore him. Ask the person closest to the celebrity where he will
be at a certain time. A men's magazine editor once assigned me to
profile an elusive politician with this warning: "Two other guys tried
and couldn't get in to see him. Maybe your working title is 'where
is So-and so today?'" When I called one of the politician's female
friends she instantly replied, "He'll be at this spot at four." I was
at that spot at four. "Joyce sent me," I said. He talked for about
an hour.

This technique is adaptable virtually anywhere. When, for
example, Brigitte Bardot was standing up writers with firm appoint-
ments, I was in Paris and went to a man who was close to Brigitte.
"No problem," he said, "let's go talk to her right now." I got a
pleasant interview with Brigitte.

Another time, in Taipei, I went to a high official in Nationalist
China's government and, consequently, was given an appointment
with Chiang Kai-shek. Though the interview was cancelled—along
with the remainder of Chiang's activities for the week—he had
someone eventually answer my written questions and gave permission
to write an article under his byline.   —*Bill Surface*

Prepare Questions — But Let the Man Talk

Prior to interviewing a subject, I endeavor to study him fairly well
and sort out my own thoughts about him and his environment. Then

I write out my questions in a fairly logical sequence. (The list of questions and the logical sequence invariably disappear very quickly; if they don't, you're in trouble.) As the first question in each area I try to phrase my question as broadly as possible so that the subject can take it in any direction he wants. If you make each question too specific, too direct, too narrow, you run the risk, I think, of ending up with an article that reflects your own preconceptions; an article that you have written in large measure before you leave home. If the guy I'm interviewing takes that opening question and goes off in a direction that never occurred to me, I figure I'm way ahead; I'm finding out what interests *him* most, rather than what interests me.

If I get a blank stare or a request to be more specific, I have a second question and, in case I draw another blank, I have a very pointed, narrow and specific third question. If I keep getting down to that third question, I'm apt to have a bad article. (Obviously, I'm not able to do this with each area, either. I just try to do it wherever I can.)

What it comes down to is this: *Let The Man Talk.* Every once in a while you get a letter from a newspaperman or a student asking how in the world you got someone to say something. The quote they cite will always be the one thing the interviewee wanted to say so badly that you couldn't have kept him from saying it at gunpoint.

I don't think you *get* people to say anything. There are some people who are constitutionally incapable of giving a dishonest answer. If you get one of them, you're lucky. Most of the time, though, the really good stuff comes in those areas they more or less introduce themselves. Again, you have to leave that opening for them to move into.   *—Edward Linn*

How to Reach an Interviewee

While telephoning is often an excellent way to conduct interviews, it is a method that has its drawbacks. Your man, for example, may be away, he may be rushed, he may not wish to speak to an unknown voice coming over the telephone. And, as has happened on occasion, he may hang up on you for one reason or another.

Next time, instead of telephoning, send a night letter. No one ignores a telegram. It not only gives the interviewee a chance to think about matters, but it gives you the opportunity to express your needs succinctly. The night letter, in fact, is an excellent vehicle for setting up further interviews, either in person or via telephone.

—William Lynch Vallée

More on Reaching Hard-to-Get Interviewees

In those cases where the telephone call is the only feasible or practicable means of reaching a hard-to-contact source, don't be put off too easily by subordinates to the one you're attempting to reach. This is particularly true in the case of celebrities.

For example, I was once assigned to do an article on Charles Laughton while he was still living. When people telephone stars like this, their press agents have a very marked tendency to say the celebrity is too busy. Ignore them. At the time I took the assignment mentioned above I was writing for six movie books and was a movie reviewer on all studio lists. Nevertheless, RKO kept stalling me, saying that Mr. Laughton was much too busy. Fortunately, I knew he was staying at the Gotham in New York City, so I simply called that hotel and asked for Mr. Laughton. He answered his phone and after I explained my problem he suggested that I come over immediately. I spent the afternoon with him, got a crackerjack interview and had sherry with the star and his delightful actress wife, Elsa Lanchester.   *—William Lynch Vallée*

Handling the Reluctant Interviewee

In getting a balky or hostile subject to see me, I usually don't press because I recognize the right of anybody NOT to be interviewed. However, if the subject is crucial to a story about someone else (I would not do a piece in which a hostile interviewee was the main subject), I do make some attempt. My usual procedure is to tell him that since he will be in the story anyway, for the sake of accuracy I would much prefer to get his statement firsthand. A corollary technique is to assure him that he will see—or be told by phone —the exact quotations that will be attributed to him.

To get balky subjects to talk once an interview has been granted, I find that, with exceptions, the same technique I ordinarily use in interviewing is usually effective; that is I try, insofar as possible, to inject none of my own views and as little of my own personality as possible, once the initial amenities are observed. If all goes well, I eventually become as close as possible to a faceless recorder of information. In this context questions are asked with the intent of keeping the flow going and are as brief as I can make them. (There are times, of course, when different stances are necessary. But for long profiles, which I mostly do, I've found the unobtrusive approach works well.) With balky subjects, this kind of blending-into-the-furniture style seems, in time, to allay whatever anxieties or suspicions they had.

All of this seems elemental and yet I've seen interviewers who can't resist inserting themselves so forcefully that the subject gets thrown off the track and there is soon a discussion and even a debate. The result is apt to be less productive of usable material, though perhaps stimulating to the writer's ego. (Unless, of course, you're writing a running dialog or debate; then that's the sensible technique.)
—*Nat Hentoff*

Getting Celebrities to Talk

Getting the quotes exactly right in an interview is less important than catching the flavor and color of a personality, knowing him as thoroughly as possible.

The experienced interviewer reads everything written about the person before seeing him, sometimes also talks to his friends. This enables him to come prepared for any unexpected turn his talk takes. It also saves him from asking routine questions that waste time and bore the interviewee.

You have to listen with complete concentration. This is necessarily flattering. Katherine Squire, the gifted Broadway actress, once told a young performer, "On the stage when you listen, *really* listen. You can't fool anybody by trying to look as though you were listening."

If you have any reportorial gift, you will develop the knack of remembering the important points in what you've previously read about the man. Write them all down ahead of time, study them, figure out what more of interest he *could* have said on various subjects. If you do all this, and care enough, you will not misunderstand or misquote him.

Never forget who the star of the interview is. Don't talk about yourself just because he politely asks you a few questions. The late John Wayne and other movie stars have complained to me that previous interviewers were too interested in talking about themselves. That is for fans and the birds. Don't act like a fan. Almost everybody enjoys being interviewed, even those who behave coyly about it and give you that "Oh, who cares about little old me" line.

I remember what happened some years ago when I went to Hollywood with an assignment to interview the late Gary Cooper. His press agents told me that no one had been able to get a publishable interview with Coop for ten years. I insisted on trying. This was at lunch in the Warner Brothers commissary, which is like trying to interview somebody during a hurricane.

I talked to the big fellow for a few minutes and saw what the press agents meant. I was cooked unless I thought of something that would interest him. What I thought of was that although everybody loved Coop, he was an actor. So I said, "Mr. Cooper, everybody says you hate to talk. I love to talk. Why don't you, under your byline, interview *me* and I'll print *that* as our story."

He laughed and gave me a story that had never been published before, a wonderful story of how he got into his car between pictures, visited little towns, talked to ordinary people, found out what they were interested in, how crops were doing, what pictures pleased them or annoyed them. The point of my interview-story was that Hollywood always marveled at Gary Cooper's down-to-earth quality. He'd arrived in Hollywood with it. The secret trips helped him keep that quality through all his years of stardom.

—*Charles Samuels*

Presenting Your "Company Credentials" as a Freelancer

Probably more than a few freelancers have been, like me, annoyed by the persistent question, "And what company are you with, Mr. Watkins?" This happens, obviously, when you call to interview some organization man who is shielded by a battery of outside receptionists and secretaries.

Being a freelance writer, you cannot honestly say you are from the FBI and there are times when it isn't appropriate or natural to mention the name of the magazine for whom you're writing your article. Or it may entail a complicated explanation to tell a perfectly pretty but vacuous young lady that you're a freelance and writing an article, etc.

My standard answer, therefore, is that my company is Watkins and Watkins, Inc. And on rainy Thursdays and cloudy Fridays I sometimes say with a perfectly straight face—I've built up a lot of experience at it—that I'm with Watkins, Watkins & Johnson or Watkins, Watkins & Waxy, depending upon the interrogator's mien. This answers the question, gets a perfectly satisfactory and often impressed response from the cute but staunch little number at the telephone board and she immediately puts through my request to see my source.

When I'm out interviewing people or doing research and somebody asks for my company name, I'm always delighted to please and give them one. I also put down the same company name when I register at hotels and motels. It seems that a freelance writer, like a single man, is suspect in the U.S.A. So simply assuming the shawl of free enterprise and providing yourself with a company name can often make all the difference in the world in the reception you get and in having doors opened for you.   —*Art Watkins*

Cross-Interviewing

In trying to get both the truth and color of a personality it is essential to see him from many angles. To re-create episodes and scenes from his life, it is not enough to know how they appear to him, but also how they figure in the recollections of those persons involved with him at the time.

To put this technique into effect the author must become both moderator and actor. As moderator he feeds the person he is interviewing just enough information to evoke a stream of thought and recollection. As an actor, the author has to react to the scene to stir reactions in the other through empathy.

Sometimes, however, the writer must withhold rather than feed clues. This keeps the interviewees from knowing what others have said and puts him wholly on his own. The writer is thus able to get different versions of the same story.

Usually I like to interview the friends and relatives of my subject first. This makes it possible for me to absorb the salient facts and feelings with which I can come armed to interview the principal. This makes the difference between asking general questions and asking concrete ones.

This method also serves as an ice-breaker. When, for instance, I was doing an article about Sargent Shriver, head of the Peace Corps and of the President's anti-poverty program, the first thing I said to him was, "I bring you greetings from two of your old teachers at Canterbury."

Sargent Shriver looked at me in consternation and delight. I had been at his old preparatory school recently; he had not. I had delved into his past by talking to his teachers and this filled him with nostalgia. Before I knew it, he was asking me questions about his old school and we were talking like human beings. The formal interview had been abolished before it began. The result was that by the time I left I not only had personal and human material for my article, but I also found myself involved in a book about Shriver.

—*Flora Rheta Schreiber*

Ask Your Subject to Describe a Typical Day

Ever find it difficult to defrost a cold subject when you are interviewing him? Getting the subject to disclose anecdotal meat not only is an occupational hazard of our profession, but can be damnably frustrating. Whenever I sense that the interview has hit an unresponsive snag and I am stuck with an inarticulate interviewee, I resort to a gambit which has worked wonders. I simply say, "Mr. Jones, could you describe to me what you do on a typical day in your life, from the moment you get up until going to sleep at night?"

Brother, does this question move mountains! When I asked this of Fleur Cowles, the lady began, "First I ring for my maid to bring me breakfast in bed. Then she gives me the mail and I dictate answers to my secretary. Then I tell her what to do that day, what to order from the store, a light to be fixed in the parlor and so forth. Then I take a cab to my office and read *Time* in the taxi . . . etc."

Another VIP of whom I asked this question told me how he always spends his lunch hour in the public library, reading out-of-town newspapers. I think you get the message by now; when you cast your bread upon the waters via this query, it's apt to come back buttered and topped with caviar.   —*Mort Weisinger*

Finding Anecdotes on Subjects You Can't Interview

The best device for obtaining anecdotes is, of course, being amidst the action. But there are subjects whom a free-lance writer cannot interview. I experienced this problem while writing an article on the probable successor to Russia's Nikita Khrushchev and, after getting intelligence pointing to Khrushchev's protege, Leonid Brezhnev, studied his speeches and background. Still, I needed some recent insight into Brezhnev's personality. While reading translations of the Soviet press, I noticed that in 1963 Brezhnev had greeted a group of American scientists in Moscow to discuss peaceful uses of atomic energy. I contacted Dr. Glenn T. Seaborg, chairman of the U. S. Atomic Energy Commission and, though I seldom show a third person piece to anyone, promised to let Seaborg approve any remarks attributed to him. Dr. Seaborg, who had talked for three hours with Brezhnev, was very cooperative. While the article was in proof form, Brezhnev unexpectedly helped force out Khrushchev and, after the lead was rewritten, resulted in the first profile of the new boss of Russia's Communist Party. —*Bill Surface*

Establishing Rapport with Chit-Chat

When preparing for an interview, I always read as much as I can on the subject beforehand so that I can talk the person's language to some extent and will know somewhat better what type of questions to ask. Also, it saves time if you don't need to listen to what is already available in print; the greatest value of personal interviewing lies in getting what you *can't* find in print.

I start out, however, as if we both had all the time in the world. This is to establish rapport, to get the feel of the interviewee's personality and to put him at ease with me. Only after some preliminary chit-chat apparently irrelevant to the subject do I get down to the point.

Whether I'm writing an exposé or a plug, I take the attitude that I'm completely in sympathy with what my informant believes and want to tell the story as he wants it told. This doesn't involve lying. It simply consists of a respectful, open-minded listening to his viewpoint. —*Edith M. Stern*

Laying Cards on the Table in "Hard-Nosed" Reporting

I don't like to think that I'm *really* the type, but over the years I've done some hard-nosed reporting-investigating. I first wrote an exposé of Klan operations at St. Augustine for *Life;* next a lead piece called, "The Birmingham Bomber," for *The Saturday Evening Post;* then I was hired by NBC-TV to check out rumors of the Kennedy assassination.

This, more often than not, has put me in the position of wanting dope from people whose views I do not share—southern cops, for example.

For what it's worth, here are some of the methods I use. First, I lay my cards on the table, tell my subject exactly what I want and why I want it. I don't try to kid him or deceive him. I make a complete declaration of it, no matter how much I know he may not like the lines of my approach. The point is, of course, that they're not that dumb; they're going to find out anyway, listen to your phone conversations, follow you, etc., as they do especially in Mississippi and Alabama.

Second—and this is maybe the most important thing—I don't ask for anything I don't need. I try to figure out before an interview what it is exactly that my subject knows that I really want to know. I don't go fishing. In fact, I'll settle for very little. I'll take just one small fact if my subject will give it to me. I'll pick up my notebook, thank him and leave. I never press or try to outwit. Even if my subject is dumb, he is not so dumb as to be unaware of what is happening.

The point, naturally, is that I can always go back. My technique is to take this one fact and use it to get something out of the next fella. It's like weaving a tapestry out of short threads. And no one of the guys feels himself responsible for having given me the whole story.

The result is that now I have a kind of network of cops (high and low) who will give me specific answers to the kinds of specific questions I ask.   —*George McMillan*

Respect Your Interviewee's Time

People you interview are generally busy people. A writer's promptness and consideration of their time pays off. Normally, when I call a subject to make an appointment for an interview, I tell him how much time I need. I try to arrive on time with my interview planned in advance.

When my time is up I mention it and act as though I am about to leave. In most cases the subject continues to talk and often my best material comes during the "overtime." That happened to me while interviewing Dave Garroway. He was so pleased at my respect for his time that he continued to talk and I dropped a few more anecdotes into my notebook. One of those anecdotes gave me an extra bonus. It did not particularly fit the story I was doing, but I sold it to *Reader's Digest* for their "Laughter is the Best Medicine" department.

—*Frank P. Thomas*

Catching the Hostile Subject Off Guard

While interviewing, it's not unusual to have your subject suddenly clam up if he sees you jotting down a quote he has made on a touchy or controversial point. I avoid the pitfall this way: when the subject lets something slip that I sense he might retract on reflection, I appear to pay no interest whatever, keeping my pencil far away from the notepad. However, I do impress his quote or fact in my memory and wait until he switches to another topic. Then, as soon as he says something platitudinous—something I have no interest in whatever— I jot down the controversial remark he made earlier. The subject thinks I'm quoting him on something he wants to be quoted on and is not alarmed. This is an effective way of throwing the subject off guard and eliciting information that might otherwise be given only on an "off-the-record" basis.

Usually it's important for the writer to keep control of an interview, but there is one time when it's best to let the subject take control, I've found. That's when you're interviewing a relatively hostile subject who can be expected only to mouth denials under any normal interrogation. Since flat denials usually make pretty dull reading, it sometimes pays off to let the subject chart his own course for the interview.

For example, on a *True* assignment I interviewed Joey Glimco, a notorious hoodlum who had been involved in some labor conflict in connection with his job as a Teamster's official. I raised an initial few points made by Glimco's opposition and saw that he was going to respond only with straight denials, so I gradually let him take control of the interview and ramble in areas of his own choosing.

In the course of the afternoon he said and did some very funny things which he would never have done under conventional interrogation. When it came time to write the article, these were the things that I used—to very good advantage—in drawing a portrait of him.

—Charles Remsberg

Cracking the Difficult Interview

Of the three basic methods of interviewing—listening and remembering, taking notes, using a tape recorder—I prefer the tape recorder when its use is possible. It has several advantages. If you're doing a first person article or book (especially book) it's absolutely essential. You can get the stuff down in the guy's (or gal's) own words, or at least how he expresses himself so you can simulate his words. You know what he would say and how he would say it.

Other advantages to using tape are that you avoid misquoting or mistaking his meaning. You don't forget the meat of his story. And, if he claims misquotation (highly unlikely, since he has to OK the copy if it's for first person anyhow) you have the evidence right in his own words. For that reason alone I like to use tape, even if the interview is for a third person piece. With the latter he won't see the copy, but you still have recorded evidence that you haven't misquoted him.

Some people freeze up with a tape recorder, but usually they come around. They're just as likely to freeze up when they see a notebook. And if you don't use either, you're taking a chance of misquoting because most people's memories—like mine—aren't infallible.

The only time in recent years I had to remember was when I did the Cape Coral land hard-sell piece for *Life* in which my wife cooperated. We both carried notebooks, but couldn't use them in the presence of the guys trying to sell us. We solved it by claiming frequent kidney calls. About every half hour one of us went to the nearest restroom where we madly scribbled notes on material still fresh in our minds.

I never try to interview anybody without finding out all I can first about the interviewee and his subject. I try not to ask questions I can find the answer to elsewhere. And—although I don't always succeed—I try very hard to ask my question, then shut up. It's a temptation to insert a comment or ask another question or demonstrate what I think I know before he has finished his answer. With interviewing it's as important to know when to shut up as when to talk. You seldom learn anything talking, anyhow. Besides, your subject might digress to better stuff than you had thought of yourself if you let him talk.

I also try to find out what will stimulate the interviewee. I once interviewed a rough movie star by starting with a gag I was told he'd find funny (which he did) and then asked just one question that got him off on the story of his life. I didn't have to say another word.

I once got a very shy 17-year-old girl to talk about the story I was after by finding out her favorite school subject, doing a quick brush-up job and showing I knew a little (only a very little, but it sounded like a lot) about it.

She had given a hip bone to a younger sister for a bone transplant about a year before I saw her. I couldn't do the piece until both girls had recovered and enough time beyond that elapsed so we could be sure the recovery was permanent. I took the girl and her mother to dinner twice and her mother did all the talking. I then took her alone to lunch and I did all the talking. I had all the facts by then, but I couldn't get the guts of the story without shaking the kid loose from her shyness.

The day after we had lunch I took her to lunch alone again. I asked her what her favorite school subject was and she said English (she was a high school senior). I asked her what phase she liked best and she said she was going through the school reading list. I asked her her favorite books and she said she had just discovered the Russian novelists and thought they were wonderful, had finished *Anna Karenina, War and Peace* and was now working on *Crime and Punishment.*

That was the first time she had volunteered anything. Up until then the only talking she had done was in direct answer to my questions. She was a very pretty girl but, because of her failure to communicate, had seemed dull and utterly negative as a personality. But now her face lighted up and she began to show signs of animation.

Then I asked her what she liked about the Russian novelists and she said, "They don't just describe what happens. They tell how people *feel* when it happens."

"Which," I said, "is exactly what I've been trying to get you to do for four days."

And she gave me a hell of a story.   *—Al Hirshberg*

Knowing When to Quit Interviewing

I always know when I'm through interviewing on a piece. It's when I feel bored stiff with the answers I'm getting; that is, when I seem to be getting virtually the same old answers from everyone I question; and especially when I can't seem to think of any new questions to ask. If I'm out of town, this is when I grab a cab back to the hotel, start hurling things into a suitcase and call the airport for a reservation on the next plane home.   *—Gerald Walker*

For Portraits in Depth, Establish Rapport First

When I do an in-depth portrait of an individual involved in a dramatic narrative—a teen-aged drug addict, woman alcoholic, unwed mother—I often spend many hours, perhaps a day or two, simply talking to the person or members of the family without even mentioning the problem. Only when I feel we have established real rapport do I enter upon the subject at all. I have known reporters who would begin an interview as follows: "We've only got a couple of hours, so let's skip the amenities and get right to it. Now, that time you murdered your baby, what was going through your mind . . .?"

The other way adds days to your research time but you come away with an infinitely better story. Not only does your subject tell you more but, when you understand him as a person, you are better able to evaluate what he tells you. —*Lester David*

How to Overcome the Resistance of Interviewees

When an interview presents perils for the interviewee, I adopt a kind of therapeutic role in which I provide as much reassurance for him as I can muster. The least effective role for the writer when an inter viewee is scared or uneasy is to be a tough, swashbuckling inquisitor. What I try to do is assure him of my good will and sympathy. During the interview I even try to identify with his situation though I may privately disapprove of what he is or represents. (For example, in talking with deans or presidents of colleges, I pretend for awhile to adopt an administrator's view of things, though I am essentially anti-bureaucratic.)

In the meantime, my interviewee is warming up and relaxing. (Nothing is more effective towards those ends than getting someone to talk about his work.) In certain situations I will even offer certain guarantees—such as promising to send a copy for clearance of the section of the article dealing with him. I find that such a promise almost always overcomes resistance, since the interviewee feels that he can control the material.

But the most effective technique is to show sympathy, approval and warmth. In other words, a good nonfiction writer has to be something of a method actor, capable of working his way emotionally into almost any kind of role. The drama of this situation, to be sure, comes when you decide that you have done enough role-playing and it is time to challenge your interviewee; in short, to play inquisitor. That is the moment of truth in any confrontation between writer and interviewee.

For example, in talking with a dean of women in connection with a college portrait, I was all sympathy and warm rapport as she described the agonies and vexations of her job. Yes, the girls *can* be difficult, I agreed. They *are* terribly vulnerable. They *need* the guidance of an older person, etc. Then I sprang the question I really came to see her about. Is it true, I asked, that somebody in authority had written to the mother of a girl who was known to be dating a Negro boy? By this time there was too much trust built up between us for her to be anything other than straight with me. Indeed, she did try to resist the question, but I persisted. There was little pretense of sympathy now. I simply wanted the answer to the question.

I got it.   *—David Boroff*

Listen, but Watch for Non-verbal Clues, Too

To me, the most enjoyable part of research has always been the interview. When I was teaching the nonfiction course at the University of Indiana summer writers' workshops, the thing that struck me most in conversations with students who wanted to write articles and books was their great reluctance to interview people. Not the Secretary of State or a head of government, but somebody like the outstanding barber in town. I realized a great many people are afraid of interviewing.

Yet, interviewing is not too different from any situation in which people meet, whether old friends, casual acquaintances or strangers. And if you get ten free-lance writers to interview the same subject, they will probably each come away with different things. They would ask different questions, react to different verbal stimuli, hear different connotations. Yet it's not so hard to get people to talk. Actually, most people are eager for the chance. Often they will tell embarrassing things. The reason, I think, is that nothing is real to us until we have put it into words—told it to somebody else. The problem of getting people to talk really isn't a problem at all. But to do it you must listen carefully and not be thinking of what you plan to say next. If you are listening and really interested and excited, you will get a good interview. If you are bored or look at your watch, your subject notices it very quickly.

Aside from getting the subject to talk, I also try to stay alert to other clues, non-verbal, about personality. I was interviewing a woman of 25 a few weeks ago. She was applying orange lipstick to match her quite garish orange nail polish. She put the lipstick on cleanly, but then smeared it carelessly so that it discolored several of her teeth. I drew certain conclusions about this woman. If she had implied, for example, that she was a neat housekeeper, I would have wondered about that and felt more investigation was called for.

Finally, there's no one way to get a good interview. Some writers barge in like the guy in "Front Page" and start shooting questions and get terrific results. Others rub one foot against the other, are shy and modest, yet get terrific results. If I have any technique it is that I just forget about technique. I simply try to talk with my subject as though he were somebody I have always enjoyed talking with. Sometimes I talk a lot myself—about things that interest me, my own life, my own problems. But when the other person is speaking, I listen.   —*Maurice Zolotow*

Let Your Interviewee Talk and Don't Trust Your Memory

Of interviewing techniques, I have found the "passive" approach best. Let the other guy do the talking; steer him gently once in a while. With few exceptions I've never found a person who doesn't like to sound off, if you give him the chance. Throw an occasional question or comment into the hopper—let the other guy do the rest.

My practice is never to condense or alter a quote. If it isn't usable as is, don't use it. This is out-of-context quoting in its worst form.

NEVER trust your memory. Write everything down. You can toss it aside later if necessary.   —*Sid Ross*

Taking Notes Directly on the Typewriter

When the interviewee and occasion allow, I take notes directly with a portable typewriter. My questions are already typed out, one per page (prepared ahead from the previous day's notes, if it's a book), and I slip in the page, type that information only, take it out and put in the next question page. This saves cutting up and organizing material later.   —*Beth Day*

Three Ways to Encourage More Talk

When interviewing, it pays to appear to be on the same side as your subject, even when you are not. This requires a little deception on your part, but if you appear too antagonistic, your interviewee may refuse to talk. From SMW member Ted Berland I picked up a good method of asking prying questions without offending. He begins his antagonistic questions by saying: "If you'll allow me to be the devil's advocate. . . ." With that preface you can virtually insult the guy and chances are he won't get mad.

Another method of eliciting information is use of the studied silence. After your interviewee has finished one trend of thought, don't ask another question. Just look at him quietly. Often he will become embarrrassed and either give some additional material or introduce a related matter. Of course, sometimes he simply stares back and then it's up to you to move the interview along with more questions or comments.

One way of obtaining anecdotes is to recite an anecdote you have already collected on the subject at hand. Often the person you're interviewing will respond to this challenge by trying to top you with a still better example.   —*Hal Higdon*

An Eye for Detail, an Ear for Dialog

I recognize every person as my superior in some manner. With this attitude, I find it easier to communicate and to induce the other fellow to talk. I never compete with the experts. Like any reporter, I endeavor to background myself as thoroughly as possible in order to win confidence and to appear reasonably knowledgeable, but at all times I'm a pupil at the feet of the master. I go out to report, not to argue—as altogether too many interviewers do these days!

Two things are vital to the art of interviewing: you must develop *an eye for detail* and *an ear for dialog.*

It's often the little things that add up to a good story. I remember a few years ago visiting a camp for the handicapped in the Pacific Northwest where I was at first depressed by the spastics, blue babies and other afflicted. Nothing was happening. And then, one night at campfire, I watched a crippled lad trying to fork his wiener on a stick. His twisted hands wouldn't work and the sweat beads stood out on his forehead. Abruptly he did it and with a wonderful look of triumph, he lisped, "First time I ever got a wiener on a stick!"

And I had my story—a series of little triumphs that added up to a great accomplishment in rehabiltation of these crippled youngsters.

You need to listen to *how* people talk, too.

There was Jim Shoulders, "Businessman on a Bull," who made $30,000 to $50,000 a year riding those ornery Brahma bulls in the rodeo ring. First time I visited Jim's ranch near Henryetta, Oklahoma, the cowboy was on the phone arguing with the Internal Revenue Service. Finally, after an interminable talk, he slammed down the receiver, swung around to me and exploded:

"Them Internal Revenue boys have got me spinnin' like an ol' bull!" Then he grinned, displaying teeth liberally laced with gold inlays where "a bull stepped in my mouth once," and we got on with the interview.   *—Paul Friggens*

Asking Provocative Questions

Here are some tips from the city room of the *New York Post* as promulgated by Mrs. Dorothy Schiff, former editor-in-chief and publisher, for guidance in eliciting human interest for news features. Ask your subject some of these questions:

What person influenced you most in life?

What book, if any?

What do you believe about people—can they be changed for better or worse?

What do you do for relaxation?

What was your greatest opportunity?

These and similar queries can help reveal the guiding forces that shape and drive the person you are sitting with vis-a-vis for your personality story.   —*Beatrice Schapper*

Chapter Six

TAKING NOTES

Paper-Pinching — The Most Wasteful Economy

Putting too many notes on one sheet of paper is the most foolish and wasteful attempt at economy for a writer. When one sheet carries several notes on different topics, he will usually be forced to rewrite some of these notes (or all of them) later on separate sheets. It is far more economical, when taking notes originally, to turn to a fresh page in the notebook or to slip another sheet into the typewriter, so that each note on a given topic can be placed in your files where you want it. When you are writing a manuscript of considerable length, hours can be lost in searching for a note you remember having made but which remains lost somewhere below another one filed under a different heading.

Even if you were to use up a full ream (a 500-sheet package) of yellow copy paper in being extra paper-generous on a long project, as compared to being miserly, the cost out of the pocket would amount to about $6.00. Note we said "use up," not waste. The saving in time and annoyance would be many times that if you value your time and temper at all.　　　　　　　　*—Alden Todd*

Typing Notes Marathon Style on Adding Machine Tape

As many writers do, I take notes in a cryptic, wrist-breaking longhand. (Why so few American reporters know shorthand and so many English ones do is a mystery—I would make it a required course in schools of journalism.) But when it comes to transcribing these raw notes. I part company with most of my colleagues. I cannot accept as necessary the strain required by typing a separate card for every sentence or two of interview, not to mention the waste of cards. Yet, how else can they be broken down for sorting and logical use?

Instead of cards, I use a roll of adding machine paper, 3½ or 4 inches wide. After each notation I skip a few spaces, note the source, add an asterisk in the middle of a line and move on to the next item. When I am done I have a few miles of tape which my little girl then tears into slips by ripping against a straitedge placed over each asterisk. If you don't have a little girl, a little boy will do the job just as willingly and an older one can be coerced. Arrange the slips as you would cards.   —*Robert Bendiner*

You'll Never Regret Learning Shorthand

Many times I am asked if shorthand is important to the writer. You can bet it is. I once took the trouble to learn shorthand and I've never regretted it. For one thing, it saves time. It also permits me to hold an interview that is more nearly like a relaxed conversation without awkward, mechanical pauses. If there's anything that distracts the subject it is his saying something and then watching the writer go through contortions getting it down in longhand. That dead spot can hurt the flow of your interview. Usually I'm through putting it down just seconds after he says it. This, I find, surprises and pleases a busy man and gives him the feeling that he is dealing with a professional, which in turn makes him more willing to talk.

Another benefit of my shorthand is that in getting it down fast I have more time to think about the next question. Then, of course, there is accuracy. I've rarely ever had a quote challenged after it appeared in print. Though I use shorthand (Pitman) I don't by any means take down every word the man says. I take key words and phrases down in shorthand just as many of my colleagues do in their own contrived shorthand using letters of the alphabet. However, I have come to sense when a man is going to make a key statement. When that happens, I take down every word.

—*Frank P. Thomas*

Typing Your Longhand Notes Jogs the Memory

I take terribly sloppy notes, so it's worth it to me to type out what I've handwritten before I begin writing the article. There are two reasons: first, because it's easier to read and avoid error and, second, because it prods my memory to fill in the things a source said that I didn't jot down during the press of an interview. In doing this, quite frequently you can come up with notes that are astonishingly close to total recall.   —*Gerald Walker*

Taking Notes on a Wire Service Roll

I have found that in handling a major magazine project—one that involves a great deal of note-taking from many sources—the use of a wire service (such as UPI or API) carbon roll in your type-writer can save a great deal of time when you're ready to do fitting and pasting of those notes for organization of the article. What happens is that the roll is fed continuously into the typewriter as the notes are transcribed from the written form. Then, particularly if this roll is already fitted with a carbon, snippings can be re-arranged in such a manner that another draft can more easily be put together. I have found this preferable to trying to rearrange pages and pages of typewritten notes into an organized form.

—*Milton Golin*

Free Note Paper

An excellent source of paper for taking telephone notes is the agency that sends "news releases" on heavy quality paper. I draw a line down the middle of the printed side of each sheet to show it is a discard, unstaple the works, and keep it handy on the desk. During phone interviews, this heavy paper makes writing—and correcting—easy; it doesn't tear. When I get ahead of my inter-view needs, I find it makes excellent second sheets for carbon copies of letters and articles.   —*Ruth Boyer Scott*

Using a Small Looseleaf Book for Note-Taking

I prefer taking my notes in a 3½ x 6-inch ruled looseleaf notebook with the spiral wire on top rather than at the side. Such a notebook fits easily into a suit jacket's inside breast pocket without bulging and replacements are readily available everywhere. After finishing an interview, I tear that set of pages from the notebook (with the first page as a heading page), and I staple them together. Anything important I underscore or star heavily while I'm taking notes; later I mark these sections with red crayons. This keeps everything from one interview together in a neat, easily-referred-to package. These notes are later typed up before writing. In typing, the notes are sometimes amplified; or sometimes typed selectively, using only a few especially relevant quotes.   *—Gerald Walker*

Use Looseleaf Notebooks and Circle Dates in Red

Consider taking notes in ordinary looseleaf notebooks rather than on conventional library cards. Advantages: once sorted, your notes do not get mixed up, even if the whole stack falls from a second story window; a notebook is easier to carry than a stack of cards held together with an always slightly frayed and just-about-to-break rubber band; large sheets of note paper are just as cheap as cards and there is no extravagance in using a whole sheet for a five-word note; generous space on each sheet leaves room for later handwritten comments, key words, suggestions to yourself for further research, references to other related notes, etc.; looseleaf sheets are large enough to give room for the occasional lengthy note; when the job is finished, the whole bundle of notes, arranged in proper order, can be tied together with a bit of string and filed flat in a small space in an ordinary letter file, whereas a bundle of note cards is as handy to file as a double-bed mattress.

Keep a red ballpoint pen handy and circle *every* date in your notes to make them conspicuous. Dates are the skeletal structure of historic research and you will save hours of fumbling if they are quickly visible.   *—Bern Keating*

Make Sure Notes are Legible

For interviews in person, I always carry my looseleaf notebook with plenty of 5½ x 8½-inch paper. Name, date, phone, address, subject are pre-typed at the top of the first page. I use the smaller book because I have found larger ones too heavy to support on my left hand under certain conditions—during a one-hour tour afoot, for example. If notes might become illegible because ideas are flowing rapidly or because of weather or terrain hazards, I use every other line. This makes my notes much easier to read later on.

For "good" notes I'm sure to be using, I type out my handwritten notes as soon as possible, while my memory is still an aid. For more dubious notes, I staple the pages together and hope I'll be able to read them should I need the information later. Time is income to a freelance writer. He can't afford to waste it writing up notes he may not use. *—Ruth Boyer Scott*

Keep a Carbon of Typewritten Notes

If your handwriting is not good (and even if it is), it's wise to type out all notes while fresh in your mind, if possible, immediately after an interview. Many find it advantageous to make two copies —an original and at least one carbon of the typed version. One copy is kept intact, with everything from a single source together. The other is cut apart, sometimes in fragments as small as a sentence, and sorted by subject—maybe with material from a score of sources. If one of these fragments is lost or questioned, you can go back to the intact copy. *—Tom Mahoney*

Clandestine Note-Taking

I've used a number of methods for taking notes other than with the tape recorder so as not to be too noticeable. One is to attach a lead pencil point to the ring on my right hand and to scribble either on my cuff (laundry bills are not too high because this doesn't happen too often) or on the inside of a match book cover. There is also the method of leaning over as you are seated with your left hand holding a small note pad underneath the upper part of your right leg and your right arm stretching over the other side of your right leg so what you are doing is keeping notes underneath your right knee and out of view.   —*Milton Golin*

Chapter Seven

ORGANIZING RESEARCH MATERIALS

Quick Visibility for Notes

The two best tools for organizing notes, to my mind, are scissors and stapler. Instead of fussing with cards or indexing notebooks, I save hours by simply scissoring up my original scribbled and typewritten notes and stapling them on long (legal-sized) sheets of paper according to topic. Of course, I mark the topic at the head of each sheet in big crayoned letters so I can refer to it quickly. With all notes about a particular facet of the story on the same sheet (or several sheets with the same heading), my eye can run over them at a glance and pick out what I want. Usually I spread all the sheets on a big table beside me as I write, so that all notes for the entire story are visible at once. This is especially useful when I've done many days on interviewing and research at odd times and places, so that my notes are jotted on varying shapes and sizes of paper. I don't have to transcribe them onto cards or shuffle through them to find a specific note when I need it. One short flurry of scissoring, sorting and stapling gets everything permanently arranged and visible.   *—Keith Monroe*

Organizing with Scissors and Paste

Source material for most of my articles comes from a wide variety of people and places—interviews, reports, clippings—much of which overlaps. To whittle down the stack and fix the essentials in mind, I go through the works carefully, typing out the gist of each piece of material on yellow paper. I then cut these typewritten sheets into paragraphs and even sentences, arranging them into the five or six basic sub-headings that conform to my outline, weeding out obvious duplications and finally pasting them onto long sheets of paper in as close to chronological sequence as possible. What I have now is a long, long first draft and I am able to begin at the beginning and write my way through the entire article without the need to go back to source for memory refreshment or to go digging through a great mass of material for some half-remembered quote that suddenly seems to fit a particular spot.

This system had its acid test in an 80,000-word biography of George Washington Carver for the *Reader's Digest*. My paste-up sheets ran to about 40 in number, each a foot or more in length. I spent perhaps six weeks putting them together, but I would bet that I saved twice that time when I settled down to actual writing. A tangential bonus came when those exacting *Digest* research gals began checking my sources. With every, "Where-did-you-get-that?" I had only to look at my paste-ups, each fact keyed to a letter source, and they had their answer.   —*Lawrence Elliott*

Take Time to Organize Carefully

To me the most important part of writing a book is not the research or the writing but the period in between, when you decide what you have gathered is complete and how it can most coherently be presented. This is the phase when I must be by myself for a few months. The writing can be done in hotels, on planes, etc., but the conceptualization requires a long, uninterrupted period for careful sifting of materials, deciding how they relate, organizing the material into chapters and then organizing the material by sections within each chapter. For my book, *The Naked Society,* I found that the various subsections of material added up to about 130 piles of research material.

Another lesson I learned: don't let anyone open the door to a room where you have 130 piles of paper if a window is open. My kinder did so, the room filled with flying papers and I had to redo a day's work. *—Vance Packard*

Keying Your Research into Your Outline

When my research on a story is completed—when the library has been sucked dry, all my interview tapes transcribed, the last of my data-requesting letters answered—I usually tend to come to a halt. By this time my curiosity has been satisfied; I know all I want to know and I'm totally bored with the subject. To get over this hump and to make sure that I get everything I want into the piece, I use the mechanical device of outlining and keying.

Here's how it works for me:

I put the story title or subject at the top of a sheet of legal-sized, lined, yellow paper. Underneath I write "Lead," then down at the bottom, "End." Big feeling of accomplishment comes here. I think of the general sequence of the story in a broad way, establish where the major components will go and drop subject heads at various points on the page.

For example, almost every piece has a history section—how whatever I'm talking about got to wherever it is now. So maybe halfway down the sheet I write "History," then perhaps two-thirds down I place "Where we are now" and maybe this is followed up by "Significance." Back at the top again, after "Lead," I may put "Who cares?" Often my major spokesman says who cares, so his name comes down a couple of lines from that head, followed by a subhead called "Personality," where later I'll tell about his warts and shifty eyes.

OK. I've got a sheet with a dozen major topics. Now I spend perhaps an hour thinking about the story and adding other points, still without checking my research.

Finally I'm ready to begin keying. I put all the background papers—interviews, other magazine articles, scientific papers—in a pile and number the topmost "1." Then I read it thoroughly, perhaps for the first time. When I come to something interesting, I make this "a" and on my outline sheet at the logical point I write in "1a" The next interesting item goes on my sheet as "1b" etc.

The next reference sheet is numbered "2," the first point "2a." By the time I've gone through the stack, I've got a yellow sheet crammed with numbers. I type it over so I'll not get lost.

Then I begin writing. For each heading I pull from my reference stack all the papers keyed as applicable, read them, then write the paragraph. If, for example, under "History," I have four references —say 4c, 5m, 7d, 9e—I pull out 4, 5, 7 and 9, read the pertinent sections, summarize and embellish them on my paper, cross out the four reference marks on my master sheet, return the papers to the stack and go on to the next point.   —*Robert Gannon*

Tape Recording Notes after the Interview

As do many writers, I find it difficult to work from sloppy handwritten notes taken during the heat of an interview. I used to spend considerable time retyping these notes before attempting to organize my article. Now I find I can save time, avoid an unpleasant chore and telescope the whole process of organization by dictating the notes into my tape recorder and having a typist prepare them for me in a special way.

While dictating, I edit and classify the notes, paragraph by paragraph, according to subject matter. Thus, I read a paragraph, decide roughly what part of the story it will fit into or what its chief subject is, then I give it a heading. At the end of the paragraph I make sure to indicate the source of the information. In dictating, I simply omit what is irrelevant or repetitive. The result is a long series of items that look like this one—an actual fragment from the 70 pages of typed notes I used for an article about women painters:

PARENTAL ATTITUDE
My family always thought that painting was okay. There was no rebellion in that de-partment. I was very encouraged. My fa-

ther was a physician—a dermatologist—
but he also painted and sketched.   Mother
was a writer,a novelist and poet.
                                        JOAN MITCHELL intvw.

I ask my typist to single-space the note, leaving a double-space between the heading and the body, a single space between the body and source reference and four spaces between items. Since no interview proceeds in an absolutely straight line, several passages relating to the same subject may be scattered through the notes. These are all assigned the same heading. By leaving lots of room between items, I am able to cut them apart and reassemble them so that all references to the same subject can be put together.

I also ask the typist to make a carbon. Thus, I wind up with one set of notes cut up and classified by subject matter and another set in which the items remain in the same sequence in which they occurred in the interview. This becomes part of my permanent file—along with the handwritten notes, which I also retain.

Dictating the notes, rather than typing them myself, costs money, but it more than pays for itself in time saved, in neatness and convenience. Most important, it makes it possible for me to do a lot of preliminary organization very early in the game.

—*Alvin Toffler*

Organizing Notes by the Numbers

When it comes to organizing material, I use a numbering system. After my research is completed, I take a legal pad and made a rough outline, leaving several lines of blank space between each major point. In this form the outline may stretch over three or four pages. Then I take my notes and other research materials and number each page. I might have 200 to 300 pages of notes on a major story. Then I read over my notes and fill out the outline, putting a few key words of anecdotes, statistics, arguments, quotes, etc., under the appropriate outline headlines—along with the page number on which the full version of this information can be found in my notes. When I'm writing and come to that point in the outline, I just have to refer to the page number and the quote or whatever is right at my fingertips. This can save a lot of work when your notes are rather scrambled, as they're likely to be after 20 or more interviews. I also find that delineating everything this way on the outline helps in plucking out the best material for the final manuscript draft.   —*Charles Remsberg*

Keeping all the Notes in Sight while Writing

When retyping my notes before writing, I make an original and a carbon of the material. One set is stapled together and kept intact. The other set I snip apart with scissors and fit the component parts —quotes, anecdotes, description, etc.—into clusters of related data. One segment may deal with a certain period in a subject's life; another may consist of various people's quotes on a given subject. Whatever the grouping, I Scotch-tape them together into long wallpaper-like sheets which I then Scotch-tape to the shelves over my desk. This gets everything out in sight at once and it's less cluttered than spreading notes out on the floor. I can see anything I want at a glance without shuffling wildly through a pile of papers. As I use one or another snippet, I either cross out the material or actually cut it out and throw it away, taping the rest together again. It also has the advantage of making your study look relatively slapdash while you're working on a piece, so that if you're at all compulsive you race to finish the article in order to restore the place to something like order again.   —*Gerald Walker*

Organize as You Go Along

Just as the tendency to over-research is a sign of a lack of confidence in one's own ability to get started with the actual writing, so is a predeliction to over-organize. These are chronic illnesses in a writer for which he must constantly ingest intellectual medicine. The approach I found helpful was to face up to the necessity of the actual writing until confronting it became a habit; after that it was no trouble. The confidence lack, of course, is deferring the writing until the last possible moment; adopting delaying tactics which bring it right up to the deadline with the same subconscious reluctance that prevents people from seeing a doctor for a cancer test. It is a sort of subconscious fear of the end result.

Anyhow, the system I evolved consisted of writing bits and pieces of an article as a means of elaborating on skeletal notes immediately after doing the research that produced them. A useable anecdote, for instance could be written as it might ultimately appear. It might be a paragraph or two or just a couple of sentences.

For example, when I was writing the article on the late Walter Winchell that appeared in the *Guide to Successful Magazine Writing* of the Society of Magazine Writers, I was overwhelmed by facts—I read the script of every broadcast for five years as only one phase of the research. There were many errors, some more important than others (which was also true of his published columns). From the many available, I actually wrote perhaps a dozen, knowing there would be a section on errors; there had to be. I set these examples aside for this purpose.

Another aspect of the man which had to be treated was his fantastic experience in the Navy. Here again, when the research on this was completed, the salient incidents were written and set aside. The same was true of his strange relationship with the FBI. The research on this was mostly done at one time, much of it with the late J. Edgar Hoover and close assistants. When done, it was composed in final draft form.

Other sections were similarly handled, but in these three examples can be seen a formula for organization. They represent major aspects for an appraisal of the man which was the purpose of the article. When the research was wholly finished, these important segments were already written and it was not difficult to organize the balance of the article around them. They certainly helped in getting over the hurdle of getting started writing, which bothers so many people doing articles. Further, it gives a lapse between first draft material and final, which makes evaluation and correction easier. By speeding up production it can mean more articles sold per year.

—*Dickson Hartwell*

Organizing Notes with Colored Pencils

Being allergic to any kind of gadget, I do not use a tape recorder, but scribble notes in a notebook. As soon as possible after the interview, while I am still able to read my own handwriting, I copy my notes onto green typewriter paper. I use green so that I don't confuse my notes with drafts of the script, for which I use white. At this stage I do not attempt to arrange my notes topically. Headings are the names of the persons I interviewed, addresses, telephone numbers, titles (or other identification) and dates.

When I am ready to write, I go through all the notes and with colored pencils make lines in the margins for the various topics. Caution: use clearly differentiated colors. Orange and pink and certain shades of green and blue, for instance, can slow things up for you. On a separate sheet I keep a key of what each color signifies.

After I use the colored pencils, I spread all the green sheets on the bed, the ironing board, my flat-topped desk, a bureau and any other spare space necessary so that I can see the colored lines at a glance. After I have incorporated the notes into the script, I cross them out.   —*Edith M. Stern*

Noting Topics at the Head of Each Sheet

Probably everyone has several methods of organizing his writing, depending on what works for a given type story. One method I often use is to read through all my notes and collected material, note high points and reminders on different sheets by topic, then pile the notes solitaire-style with the top of each sheet showing, in different piles, and proceed.   —*Alfred Balk*

Putting Notes in the Order in which they Fit the Finished Piece

I simply organize everything on 3 x 5-inch cards. After having finished all my interviews and library research, I go through my notes and put every pertinent item, every quote, every anecdote, every reference, and the like on individual 3 x 5 cards. When finished, I am usually sitting beside a stack of cards a couple of inches high. But everything important that will go into my article is on one of those cards.

Then I take the cards and start laying them out—on my drawing board, tables, sofas. I lay them out in piles according to subject matter. All the anecdotes, for example, would be in one corner. Once having spread the cards around, I begin making an outline: I. Introduction; A. Such-and-such quote, etc. As I make the outline I am reorganizing my cards into a single pile, but this time they're in the order in which the facts will be presented in the article.

Then I sit down at the typewriter with my outline on one side and my stack of cards on the other—and write. I keep turning cards as I write and when I have reached the last card, the article is finished. This sounds awfully mechanical, but it's not.

The advantage in this system is that it cuts the time it takes you to prepare that first draft. But probably more important, it really cuts the time out of the rewrite to make the second draft. Of course, you spend a lot of time preparing for that first paragraph, but I think in the long run you come out ahead.   —*Hal Higdon*

Using Large Organization Sheets to Plan an Article

For notes when researching, I use an 8 x 5-inch dime-store notebook, to the back of which I staple a stiff piece of cardboard. It fits the pocket and the stiff backing makes it easy to take notes while standing up or walking around. When all my interviewing, library work and legwork has been done, I tear the sheets from the notebook and staple them to 8½ x 11-inch paper. (For this I use old press releases, of which every professional writer has an inordinately large pile.)

Next, I go through my whole pile of notes and collateral material, underlining in red the points I find of initial or primary interest. This also includes the quotes and anecdotes that will illustrate the hard-core stuff. At the same time I consecutively number each sheet of notes and each item of collateral.

The next move is to take a sheet of paper about the size of a desk blotter and rule it, if not already lined, into four columns. General topics that seem worthwhile go into two columns, while quotes and anecdotes are put into the third and fourth (although this is just an approximation of the messy job I do). Detailed information is not spelled out on this baby blanket of a sheet, but simply indicated in brief and keyed with the page number of the material where, presumably, the matter is fully covered.

As this is being done, I draw red pencil lines between connecting points, quotes, anecdotes and statistics or otherwise indicate any relationship between facts that will help me type up a first rough draft with relative ease. I can refer quickly by number back to the source material without waste of time. (I'd found, before trying this system, that I could easily waste an hour or more hunting for an obscure fact or quote that I knew was buried somewhere in that pile—and sometimes not even find it.)

This system also quickly points up gaps in research that need further covering. In addition, the system works equally well for chapters of books as for articles.   —*Frank Cameron*

Chapter Eight

WRITING

How to Make Yourself Work

Sometimes it's hard for a writer to discipline himself. Working alone, with nobody but yourself to urge you on, you tend to grow lazy. You become a procrastinator. You tell yourself, "Well, I don't really have to do this today. I'll do it tomorrow. Today I'll go fishing." Then you hate yourself because you know you *should* have done the work today. You go back to your typewriter and stare at the sheet of paper in it, but words still don't come. You go to bed angry and frustrated, wondering if you're cut out to be a writer after all. And sometimes, when unpaid bills are mounting up, you go to bed scared.

I've been going through this sort of torment for nine years, ever since I left a staff writing job to become a full time freelance. It hasn't always been easy, but I've learned two tricks that I can play with my own psychology to force out the reluctant words. They almost always work.

1. Everybody seems to have a time of day when his mind works most clearly and efficiently. In my case it's early morning. Back in the days before I became aware of this, I used to fret over a difficult story for hours in the afternoon. One story, for *True,* dealt with the subject of husbands who run away from home and disappear. It was a tough story because several nuances of meaning, some of them opposed to each other, had to be threaded through it simultaneously. For example, the story couldn't condone the illegal practice of family

desertion; yet it had to suggest to *True's* readers (predominantly male) that it might be fun to hide on a tropical island. I spent one whole day trying to write a single paragraph. It wouldn't come. Finally I gave up, went to bed at nine o'clock, set my alarm for three the next morning. At three I got up, had a cup of coffee, sat down at the typewriter and found that my mind had apparently been mulling all the problems over while I was asleep. Words flowed like water. All the story's resistance to being written was magically gone. I wrote 12 pages by ten that morning and finished the piece the following day.

Now I habitually rise at five o'clock, sometimes four if I'm up against a deadline and really want to turn the work out. Early morning is an absolutely delightful time of day for the writer. The kids are asleep and quiet. The phone never rings. It feels as though there is nobody and nothing in the whole world but me and my story and the two of us romp down the pages together like the good friends we ought to be.

2. Long projects tend to scare me. I tremble when I sit down to start a 300-page book or even a 25-page magazine article. Sometimes, looking mentally at all those blank pages stretched out into infinity, I've become so overwhelmed that I couldn't start at all.

This happened when I was starting to write a book called *The Split-Level Trap*. I wandered around New York for two weeks, pretending to do research. Research, hell! I had all the material I needed to write the book and knew it. But the thought of writing 300 pages in six months (the publisher's deadline) was too much. The task seemed impossible.

Then, while I was sitting gloomily on one of those benches in the plaza at Rockefeller Center, a thought came to me. Six months are roughly 180 days, right? Okay, I said to myself, if you write only *two pages a day,* you'll get your 300 done with 30 days to spare.

It was like a revelation. It was magic. Why, two pages a day were nothing!

And that's how I tackled the project. Instead of looking at the whole 300 pages ahead of me, each morning I looked at only two. Of course there were days when I didn't quite make the two. On weekends I sometimes didn't work at all. But there were other, compensating days when I made as many as 20 pages and there was one glorious day when I hit 37 (my personal record, by the way).

The psychological point is that you un-scare yourself by thinking (1) how easy it is to write two pages a day and (2) how two pages a day can mount up. If you did two pages a day, you could easily write two books a year, plus a couple of magazine articles.

—Max Gunther

Music: The Positive Distraction

If all the myriad noises of the world get on your nerves and interfere with your work, I recommend a positive distraction—music. I don't know the psychological or physiological reason but I do know that when I have background music going I don't hear the children fussing, the starlings squeaking, the tires squealing . . . and I don't hear the music, either. Nor am I alone in this; apparently it's an accepted phenomenon. The trick is getting the right music. Dixieland jazz wouldn't work and neither would Beethoven's Ninth. I recommend string quartets and piano sonatas. Pile them up on the changer and forget them. You don't hear a thing.

—Booton Herndon

Heating the Brain

It used to take a long time each day to get my brain warmed up and words flowing freely. The first few hours at the typewriter produced little wordage. But eventually I found three shortcuts to trick my brain into starting work faster.

1. I begin by reading what I wrote the previous day, editing and polishing it in pencil, then retyping the pages that are most marked up. Once I'm typing, I gain momentum and the new pages come easier.

2. I schedule longer continuous periods at the typewriter when I have a long writing job to do. Instead of three or four normal-length writing days, I'll plan a couple of continuous stints from early morning until midnight or later. This isn't as tiring as it sounds. "Brain fatigue" is mostly a myth. Surprisingly, momentum becomes a major asset after about ten consecutive hours of writing; the brain is red-hot and the paragraphs pour easily. One hour's work in this stage equals three hours when the brain is cold.

3. When finally I stop, I avoid doing so at any "logical" stopping point, such as the end of an anecdote or the wrap-up of a subtopic. Instead, I quit in midsentence, part way through development of a thought. Resuming at that point next morning is easier than starting cold with a new subtopic.   —*Keith Monroe*

To Start, Start Early

Overcoming inertia? I've tried everything from autohypnosis to setting all the clocks in the house ahead four hours (the shock of waking up at 8 a.m. and discovering it's noon was supposed to send me scrambling to the typewriter). These days I simply get up early—6 or 7 a.m. It gives me a good feeling of getting a jump on the day's work. It also frequently leaves me sleepy and I end up looking out the window.

I have a friend who uses an electric typewriter as a goad to start herself working. She claims the hum of the machine reminds her that the typewriter is second-by-second using up expensive electricity for which, shortly, she will have to pay. —*Robert Gaines*

Approaching First Drafts as if they're Final

One of the shibboleths that writers too often accept without question is the necessity of rewriting—as if this were some sort of absolution that redeems their copy from hack work. I never start the actual writing of a manuscript expecting that I'll have to rewrite it before submitting it to an editor. On the contrary, I start writing in the full expectation of turning out a pearl. When I read it over and find I've missed the mark, then I revise and rewrite as extensively as seems required. But sometimes I find that the first draft is just the way I want it—which is the way I approach every first draft.

—*Joseph N. Bell*

Getting the Most from Carbons

When typing long double-spaced manuscripts, you can get maximum use from each sheet of carbon paper by starting alternate pages one line below your usual starting line. When triple-spacing, start first on the top line, start the second page one line down, third page two lines down, then go back to the top line for the fourth page, and so on. This will use your carbon evenly on its entire surface, rather than wear out a narrow band of carbon while the strip of paper between bands is unused.

You can also shift carbon sheets around, if you are using more than one, so each gets its share of hard blows from the steel keys and cushioned strokes. Then, when uniformly used up, the lot can be discarded together. —*Alden Todd*

Write Yourself a Letter

The best technique I've ever found for getting rid of stiffness in an article is to write myself a letter about the subject. If I can interest myself in it, I'm pretty sure to be able to interest others.

—*John Kord Lagemann*

Shortcut to Word-Counting

Unless a writer must meet unusually exacting space requirements, a word-count of typewritten manuscript accurate within five per cent is quite satisfactory to the editor or other person receiving it. It is a waste of a writer's time to count words one by one. A clean typing job on standard 8½ x 11-inch office paper can be closely estimated by the following table, which takes into account an average number of paragraphs ending per page, but NOT quotations of dialog or poetry lines, both of which produce large amounts of white space:

An elite (small type) machine with generous but not wasteful margins, set at spaces 15 and 85, will average very close to 300 words per double-spaced page of 26 lines. The elite machine will also average about 225 words on a triple-spaced page of 19 lines.

A pica typewriter (large type) will average about 250 words per page of double-spaced typing with margins of the same width, set at spaces 12 and 72.   *—Alden Todd*

Writing Leads in Your Head

A Seattle magazine editor asked me, "Do you have trouble getting started writing after you have all your material?"

"Occasionally."

"Then try composing your opening paragraph before you go to your desk; while you are dressing; while you are coming home from a job or elsewhere—and, if possible and desirable, write it down in your notebook. When you go to your typewriter, you whip your lead out of your notebook or memory and the rest follows."

—Ruth Boyer Scott

Using a Flat Statement in the Lead

The introduction, or lead, of an article is no place to warm up to your subject. A good way for some writers—including me—is to warm up to it in conversation with friends, being careful not to warm up so much that the talk burns out the enthusiasm. A main object of such conversation is to find the statement that seems to make ears snap to attention. When you find it, you can almost hear the snap. And when you find it, you have your lead.

It may be an abstract idea; it may be a prediction; it may be an anecdote. Whatever it is, start right out with it without warmup or delay.

In writing your lead, you don't have to heat the words with inappropriate fire if the idea is strong and legitimate. One of my most satisfying leads, which seemed just right after trying about 20 and throwing them away, was for an article for McCall's which began with one of the most passive of all phrases, "There is . . . " The opening sentence is worded quietly because its idea is compelling —and perfectly true. It said:

"There is a man in Chicago who dares to think he has discovered the biggest cause of American poverty and how his city can begin to get rid of it."

Doesn't that make you wonder what the next paragraph said?

—*Bernard Asbell*

Quit When You're Farthest Ahead

If, like myself, you occasionally experience that familiar I-can't-get-started mental block, let me suggest a technique which has been a mental life-saver for me. I frequently make it a habit to stop writing and put the cover on my typewriter when I am hitting my stride with a section of my article which is going smoothly, when all the words and ideas are flowing beautifully and *I know exactly where I'm going.* The next morning I can hardly wait to gulp down my coffee and race back to the typewriter to finish the passage which I had already thought out. Then the keys hit the sheet magically, effortlessly, and the literary punch I had blocked out previously is finalized. By this time my mental block about getting down to another day's work has dissipated and I feel that there is a tiger in my typewriter.

Some writers might object to this technique on the grounds that they prefer striking while the iron is hot and that they are risking a possible loss of spontaneity by such procrastination. All I can say is that this system works for me. I'd suggest they try making shorthand notes about what they intend to write next, then try to work from these notes the next morning.   —*Mort Weisinger*

Save Your Shave and Beat Inertia

I usually have no problem getting started writing in the morning when I'm fresh after breakfast, but sometimes I bog down in the middle of the day. So I never shave in the morning. When I find inertia settling in, then I get up and shave. There's nothing like a clean shave to make you feel sharp again, which is what the razor people always tell us on television.   —*Hal Higdon*

Chips Off an Old Writer's Block

Writer's Block is a dread disease that can strike at any time. After suffering from it off and on all my writing life, I have found it best to accept the fact that it cannot be cured totally, but one can get periods of respite by trying the following:

Write, do not talk, to your nearest confidante, spouse, bartender, analyst, whomever. Explain—*in writing*—why the world of success is opposed to you, why life in general is unfair and organized against your best interests, why you would be able to write rings around Faulkner J. Hemingcraft if only you could overcome this temporary pen paralysis. Complain, rage, seethe, sneer, indulge in whatever histrionics or vulgarities suit your temperament: the only rule is that whatever you are emoting about must be put down on paper.

As with smallpox and other diseases treated by inoculation of small amounts of the germ into the healthy body, Writer's Block can be overcome only by writing. When I read over the declaration of grievances against the universe that I have composed, I find that either (a) I am feeling better because I have sounded off or (b) I look at what I have written and think at least I can express myself better than the moronic, self-pitying, ungrammatic idiot who wrote this piece of egotistical nonsense.

So I get back to work; maybe not on the article, book or story I have been blocked on, but at work on something—perhaps ideas to file for future articles or rewriting an old piece or even trying something in a form I never have attempted (a limerick? an aubade? Once I was feeling aubade, but now I'm no longer so sad . . . .)

If you have only a small writer's block, it may be helpful to go to the public library and read collections of The World's Worst Stories (or Plays, Novels, Articles). I find this much more inspiring than reading great works. "The Stuffed Owl" is such a collection in verse, making you feel like a genius by contrast.   —*Eve Merriam*

Change of Pace
To avoid getting "written out" after spending a long day or several consecutive days of hard typing, I sometimes get away from the word machine completely for a day and do other things, including exercise and catching up on sleep, research on future articles, and correspondence. Then I resume writing.   —*Alfred Balk*

Self Deception: The Real Destroyer of Writing Time
There is plenty of time for writing, even for those who have other jobs. The item which usually is lacking is boldness and courage. Almost all of us (especially me) are frightened of writing and, unconsciously, find excuses for avoiding it. Probably this is why many authors say, "I work best under the pressure of a deadline." Really, they are lying. The truth is simply, "Now I have no more excuses to delay. If I don't get the piece in by deadline date, I'll go hungry."

Usually this "pressure of deadlines" results in less-than-best writing. The author loses the opportunity of putting the piece away for awhile and then, later, cutting and editing. He leaves this chore to the editor, then complains because the editor does what the author should have done.

One of the ways to control your time and your fright is to pretend that you, the author, have the same kind of job as anyone else; and you punch a clock. I do this by making a chart which consists of a lined piece of paper with 31 lines, one for each day of the month. Every day I write in when I started writing and when I stopped; and the total hours put in. After that, the number of words.

A glance at this chart after a week or so is a shock. One realizes how few hours have been put in and how little labor has been done.

If an author works for four hours a day, four uninterrupted hours, six days a week, he will be amazingly productive. A personal time chart will help. What happens to almost all of us (who have not acquired the regular hours habit) is that we work like crazy for one or two days and then the memory of this sustains us for the following month. Because we slaved hard for a few days, we deceive ourselves for a long period afterwards that this is a constant pace.

A chart which indicates the hours worked and the number of words written daily is a simple technique for destroying our self-deception.   —*William J. Lederer*

Across the River and into the Prose

One of the hardest things in writing is to establish a momentum to the writing so that the sentences begin to acquire a stride about them and, finally, a certain inevitability about them. Then the writing is going good.

Unfortunately an even harder thing to do is to maintain that momentum once you have seized it. Perhaps the most frustrating experience in writing is to come back to a piece of work that was going well and find that the pace of the writing is gone. All the right sounds are muffled, the rhythm is cracked, the momentum has vanished somewhere in your absence.

In recent years I have found a way around this pitfall based on a technique for sustaining momentum that I learned, improbably, from the Alaska Scouts during World War II.

During the spring thaws overland transportation was not often available in those days, and a large part of a Scout's life was spent in marching. An equally large part of the marching time was spent slipping into ice holes and muskeg mires, often up to the neck. Often a squad could spend an entire day in marching and not cover a mile.

One squad, however, consistently the best of all the squads, invariably covered far more ground than any of the other units. They did nothing that the other squads didn't do except for one thing; At the end of a day's march the squad always stopped on the near side of a stream or river.

Logic would dictate that the squad leader take his men across the river where they could build fires and dry their clothes and be dry and comfortable and ready to go in the morning.

But the squad leader, who was part Eskimo and Indian, had a better brand of logic, based on human behavior. He knew that if his men started out in the morning all nice and dry that they would spend the rest of the day taking roundabout ways and backtracking and sidestepping to avoid slipping into the ice holes and getting wet and chilled again.

If these same men, however, had to start the day by wading across the chilly river, nothing really could bother them after that. They had been baptized for the day, immersed in it; they were *launched*.

Years later I learned to apply this concept to writing. Previously I had always kept going until I found a nice place to quit. Clean and well organized and dry. And in the morning I would find it almost impossible to start again. Even when I did begin I found myself avoiding that hard work of developing a real momentum once more.

Now I make it a point to stop at the edge of the river, one that I am eager to cross. I stop in the middle of a sentence, one that I want to finish, and I stop in the middle of a paragraph, one that I am eager to finish. I have learned not to allow myself the luxury of the sense of completing anything.

In the morning I finish that sentence and then I finish the paragraph and then the page and by that time I am in the river. The current of the day before is carrying me along and I don't have to re-create the momentum, I simply hitch-hike a lift from the day before. And forgetting momentum, simply as a device to get me working again, the Alaska Scout Approach to Creative Writing is as unfailing as permafrost.

When I look back on all the muskeg morasses that have bogged me down in the past, it makes me sad. Instead of the three books I have written I might have done ten better ones. I spent a lot of my writing youth avoiding the pain of getting wet. A little late I learned how to cross the river in the morning and get into the prose.

—*Robert Crichton*

Shortening a Manuscript — "Cut When You're Tired"

Usually the first draft of a manuscript is too long and I must trim it. Then I follow advice given by the late Ray Long, legendary editor of *Cosmopolitan* in its heyday: "Cut when you're tired." First, of course, I shelve the piece for several days to forget it. Then, some evening when I'm weary and peevish, I take up the blue pencil. In this mood I find myself thinking as I read: "Get to the point, man—what are you trying to say? . . . How dull. Why leave it in?" Slashing away surplus verbiage is a relief then instead of an agony and gets done fast. But if I'd felt fresher I might have cherished every word and fought with myself for hours before deciding what to delete.

—*Keith Monroe*

Editing when Nothing Looks Good

Finding it difficult to write before two o'clock in the afternoon, I have trained myself to spend the earlier hours of the day, or some of them, editing what I have already written of a given article or chapter. This habit serves a twofold purpose: it warms me up for the day's performance and it makes certain of a far more thorough editing and rewriting than I would probably have the discipline or patience to do after the piece is finished. The practice is rendered all the more effective, for me, by the fact that nothing I have written looks very good to me in the morning and I am therefore constrained to work it over with a savagery uncharacteristic of me, I hope, in the more civilized hours of the day. Since I start from the beginning each morning, the piece is likely to have a fairly high polish before I write the final paragraph.

There is then nothing further to do but persuade my wife to type a clean copy, since I can hardly be expected even to look at the thing again.   —*Robert Bendiner*

Read Aloud to Find Awkward Sentences

In our collaboration as a husband and wife writing team, one technique we find very helpful—especially when we have just completed our umpteenth draft and hope that an article is ready for final typing and mailing—is to *read it out loud*. At a very minimum, awkward sentences shout out their warning signals when this is done. Frequently transitional phrases which don't quite bridge the gap between one idea and the next become apparent during vocal reading. Occasionally an even deeper change is suggested—a new lead, a new conclusion or a new point of view for a troublesome middle section. *Listening* to the article enables us to approach it with a kind of fresh objectivity which we are unable to muster merely by staring at those stale yellow pages—pages by then so heavily interlined that we never want to see them again. Sometimes we read it to friends, our children or each other; but it even helps to read aloud when no one is around to listen.   —*Ruth and Edward Brecher*

Letting Materials "Age" Before Writing

I learned a good lesson from Charles Ferguson of *Reader's Digest* about using notes. He told me never to try to begin writing my article shortly after I had collected all the material but, instead, to wait at least ten days and then not to look at my notes until the first draft is completed. That way I find that I don't forget what is important to include because it stands out sufficiently in my mind. For the second draft I go over my notes very carefully to fill in statistics, details I may have missed, etc.

The point is that if you try to write immediately after finishing all your notes, your view is often distorted and you get enmeshed in details rather than focusing on the salient points. But when you let your material "age" for ten days or so, the important aspects become clear and you forget those irrelevant details which can so easily clutter an article. Possibly you'll have to glance at your notes briefly for specifics, but don't really go over them thoroughly until after you have written a first draft from memory.   —*Edith M. Stern*

Keeping Ending and Lead in Mind During Research

I try to "write" the lead and ending of a story before I ever sit down at the typewriter. From the moment I begin researching I am always conscious of those two needs. If these elements click into my mind during the course of research, I feel blessed and the writing of the story becomes a little less difficult.   —*Joseph P. Blank*

If You Can't Find a Lead, You Don't Have an Article

Many years ago, my husband and collaborator, Ed, and I told the editor of *Good Housekeeping* that we had a good story for him but hadn't yet found a lead for it.

"If you can't find a lead," he remarked, "maybe you should abandon the article. There's something wrong with it."

I was doubtful at the time but, after years of experience, I think I agree with him. If your material doesn't provide you with at least one obvious lead (better yet, a choice of several), you may have a fascinating collection of facts, but you don't yet have a story. The same factors which prevent a lead from emerging are likely to prevent a publishable article from emerging later on. Put the project away until a lead does turn up. You may lose some stories altogether that way, but it's better to lose them early than after making an excessive investment of time and energy in them.

Because Ed and I feel this way, we generally start our outlines or proposals to editors with the lead we intend to use in the finished article. If we can't find a lead for the outline, we are on notice that we may have a tiger by the tail and will be unable to find a lead for the article later on. In a significant proportion of cases, the lead we use in the initial outline is the one which appears when the article is finally published.   —*Ruth E. Brecher*

The "Bar" Test in Action

I learned what a lead really is one hot summer day in Chicago when Ruth (see above tip) and I had just spent the afternoon interviewing officials of the American Medical Association. Tired and damp, we poured ourselves onto two bar stools across the street from the AMA headquarters when an equally hot, sticky man took a third bar stool next to us, mopped his brow, loosened his tie and remarked:

"What a day! I've just finished performing an autopsy on a 316-pound 16-year-old female gorilla!"

That is what I call a lead. It is the thought you break into a conversation with—the thought which summons the reader from whatever his mind has been considering and rivets his attention on what you want him to start considering.

Ever since that afternoon in Chicago, I've learned to let my subconscious dictate a lead in a very simple way. We invite friends for dinner. After the dessert I wait until everyone is buzzing about something. Then I break in with some such remark as, "Ruth and I have been working on a fascinating subject." There is a pause. Whatever comes out of my mouth next, under the pressure of justifying myself for interrupting the after-dinner conversation—that, nine times out of ten, is the lead I've been looking for. —Edward Brecher

Using Fictional Techniques in Factual Narratives

You may be able to write better, faster-paced nonfiction by utilizing fiction techniques, as I do. My own specialty is the dramatic narrative, the story of human drama in a situation. My stories, though true, contain all the elements of fiction: depth of emotion, conflict and suspense. Hence, they must be written with the dramatic values in mind.

For example, in a piece about a badly burned boy for *Reader's Digest,* the pace went like this:

The first part of the story established the scene and the problem. Would the boy survive? The middle section built up suspense and showed the struggle of the boy and his doctor to fight off infection and other complications, both physical and psychological. The boy teeters on the edge of death in a long crisis. At the climax, he weathers the crisis. The ending, then, expressed the conviction that he will go on to live a normal life.   —*Joseph P. Blank*

Finding the Spare Time to Write

In the 15 years of spare time freelancing I've had, I've overcome the frustration of finding time to do my writing by first making up my mind that my annual output will always be rather sparse. I'm satisfied when I am able to write three magazine articles a year or one book in two years. Secondly, I have learned how to be a time thief. I steal time wherever I can; in most instances from myself and my family.

I confine my writing to evenings and weekends. Usually the house is peaceful and quiet in the evenings with the children either asleep or studying. Evening is also the time when I can best rationalize my selfish attitude towards my wife. She likes to relax at such times with her knitting, sewing or just watching television. Since I have no interest or aptitude in any of these pursuits, I do not feel badly that I am stealing her time for my writing.

I still feel guilty, though, when it comes to weekends and holidays, for I insist that I have four uninterrupted hours during the day in which to write. I try to take these hours at a time of day when my presence will be least missed. An understanding wife (and wives of writers must be both understanding and lonely) is one who has learned to schedule her lengthy shopping trips for Saturday and her visits with friends or relatives for Sunday, so as to leave her husband alone with his typewriter.

When it comes to editing articles, I find that stealing time becomes easier. Using a clipboard as a portable desk, I take my article to be edited almost anywhere. I edit sitting in the car while my wife shops or visits, on a train while commuting to work, during lunch hour while sitting in a restaurant, at an open air concert, on a park bench, even in my own living room or backyard in the midst of family activity. Because editing does take a degree of concentration, I find a set of ear plugs designed for sleeping quite helpful. Engulfed in silence and lost in my manuscript, nothing will distract me—except, of course, when I'm trying to edit while on the beach in the summertime. Ear plugs just cannot drown out the bang made by a passing bikini.   —*William Kitay*

Finding the Right "Test Audience"

Editors are annoyed when a writer, whose manuscript has been sent back for revision, complains that the editors surely must be guilty of poor judgment, for the writer's wife or one of his friends found the manuscript thoroughly enjoyable.

Nevertheless, I believe a writer is wise to show his work to someone in his own backyard before submitting it. By doing so, he frequently saves himself a revision or two. There are few writers so skillful that they are able to read their own work with adequate objectivity. A test audience serves three purposes. First, it provides the writer with a general reaction to the story. Does it come off, or does it not? Obviously the writer himself has some conviction in this matter and he need not accept a negative verdict unless he has had little faith in the manuscript all along.

Secondly, the guinea pig—wife, friend or whoever—may be helpful in pointing out where, if at all, the story sags. Thus the writer knows where to tighten.

Third, the writer learns that those two or three sentences that he has labored over and thought quite elegant are really so fuzzy that the reader cannot understand what the writer is trying to say.

It is vital, of course, that the writer select his test audience with care. In a writer's circle of friends, he'll usually find someone who has the instincts of a good editor. If the writer lacks taste, he'll pick the wrong man . . . but if he lacks taste, he's in the wrong profession to begin with.

One final word: don't tell the editor that your friend thinks the manuscript is peachy. There is nothing to be gained by telling him, nor is there any point in annoying him.   —*Myron Cope*

Warming Up with an Editorial and Headlines

Getting started into a piece is certainly an individual matter. More than any other factor, I think the very act of starting is what distinguishes one magazine writer from another. My own technique is to take the position of an adversary in the topic at hand. I write a hard-hitting editorial and a dozen or so hard-hitting, eye-catching headlines. The high points are more easily focused and localized for maximum reader acceptance when put in the form of an editorial.

It doesn't really matter whether the magazine would even consider using an editorial to go with my piece. The device is useful to me in sharpening the basic idea of the piece. However, on two occasions I submitted the editorial with the article and once one of them was used to accompany the piece.

By writing out various headlines in advance, I make available to myself "rejected" headlines which might easily find their way into the phraseology of the finished article. With a piece on venereal disease for *Mademoiselle,* for example, I wrote no less than 38 sample headlines over a period of several hours as a means of building up fresh reader interest in this topic. Of these "exercise" headlines, six to eight found their way into the text of the finished product and one, of course, became the published title: "The Whisper Diseases Explode." Rejects included:

Initials of Very Dangerous
VD is Back with a Vengeance
VD Stalks Suburbia
"Good" America's Hidden Epidemic
Who are the VD Carriers?
Intimate Diseases on the Rampage
VD Streaks Past the Red Lights

—Milton Golin

Begin in the Middle if You Must, But Begin

Be a self-starting writer by just sitting at your typewriter (or pad) and writing anything at all—even the alphabet, if nothing else comes to mind. Like a stalled car being pushed, you will find that just going through the motions of writing nothings may soon start you writing the somethings that momentarily elude you.

If you can't start your article in the beginning, start somewhere in the middle. If you get stuck there, try doing some other midsection or maybe the ending. Do the pieces as they come easiest and then, when finished, put them together. You will find that "beginning terror" dwindling as you finish more and more of your article, even though you may do it like a jig-saw puzzle or from end to beginning instead of vice versa. The important thing now is to get something down on paper no matter how you do it.

Write straight through without stopping to correct every sentence several times. You may leave a lot of imperfect passages behind to be cleaned up later, but you will come through with a smoother manuscript. What's more, you'll write faster. *—José Schorr*

Would Your Leads Pass the "Bar" Test?

For many writers, choosing the lead is one of the most difficult aspects of article writing. Often the problem is not so much the dearth of possible leads but, rather, the problem of selecting the one most apt to arrest the attention of the reader. As a guideline to selecting an attention-getting lead, an old journalism professor of mine once offered the following suggestion: "Imagine yourself in a bar wanting to strike up a conversation with a fellow tippler. Would the lead you have in mind provoke his curiosity, get him to want to know more about the subject you are talking—or writing—about? If so, it's very likely a good lead for your article."

Doing an article on "Adventures in Seeing," I first wrote a lead that went like this:

> *The average person may see a forest as a great green glob or, in the fall, may notice the trees collectively in all their gorgeous red and brown colorings. But he never thinks to look closely at the trees themselves or study the details and patterns of individual leaves.*

But it didn't seem to pass the bar test. I doubted I could get much of a rise out of anybody with an opening like that. So I put that one aside and eventually came up with this:

> *Most people, even those with 20/20 vision, are half blind and don't even know it. They look but they really don't see, and so miss much of the beauty in the world around them.*

This lead, I felt, would get attention. But I didn't discard the original lead. Instead, I used it as the second paragraph, as an example of my premise in the new lead.

Of course, there's no reason for this "bar test" to be imaginary—you can actually try it out at a bar or cocktail party.   —*Carl Bakal*

What You Cut May be Salable

It's natural, in writing an article, to try to tell all you know about that particular subject, but don't. It can clutter your writing and, equally important, you may be throwing away a second perfectly dandy story.

Some years ago an eminent literary magazine expressed interest in an article on Blacks moving into previously all-white neighborhoods. I was serving on our city's Commission on Human Relations then and, as the article developed, I found myself wanting to tell all I knew about the Commission. The article got rather long but I sent it off, then didn't hear a word for months.

One particularly detailed anecdote, about how the Commission acted in a trouble spot, had dramatic time value and, as the weeks went by, I became restless. That anecdote would soon be dated. Besides, I decided, it didn't belong in the article, which was about Black neighbors and not the Commission. So I lifted it from my carbon, added more details and sent it to a liberal news magazine, titled: "How Philadelphia Stopped a Race Riot." They bought it at once. Then I had to tell the literary magazine that this particular part of my article was no longer available. They didn't like it, for it turned out they *were* planning to buy my article when they got around to it; but I apologetically offered a substitute anecdote and the article was finally published.

A few years later, after a couple of weeks in Russia, I wrote a frivolous piece on beach life on the Black Sea for a local Sunday magazine, including a lot of miscellaneous information about the Russian approach to drinking. The magazine wanted the piece but felt it was too long and asked me to cut the part about Russian drinking. I did, but the drinking habits still seemed funny so I added some more observations and sold "Vertical Drinking in the USSR" to the same literary magazine I had robbed those years ago.

Obviously none of those multiple sales made my fortune, but they made me very happy and, though I've never applied the principle of tightening a story into two in any high-paying magazine assignment, I'm sure it could often work to the benefit of all.

—Hanna Lees

Stream of Consciousness: Starting the Mental Wheels

When I begin to write an article, I take the first two or three days for "stream of consciousness" writing. Often I will dictate into a tape recorder, but I may also write in longhand or type. Research has no part in this; nor has editing. It's a process of thinking out loud. For example, when beginning to write a recent piece for *Redbook* on creativity in women, I spent these first days recording everything I knew about the subject personally—the nature of the creative impulse as I had myself experienced it, the obstacles thrown up against its expression in the life of the average woman, and so forth.

No holds barred here. It really is almost pure stream of consciousness. By the end of my two or three days, I may have fifty pages of writing. From it an outline emerges; from it also I see the direction my research and interviewing must take. *—Ardis Whitman*

Knowing When Your Article is Good

When we start something we don't really like (but it seems like a chance to get another assignment and make more money), the longer we work on it the more we indulge in self-delusion by telling ourselves that this is really turning out pretty well and that we are interested in it.

There is a quiet second voice we could listen to which is saying, "Nuts; this is rotten and it isn't going to work." But we don't let that voice speak up very often. If we did, I think we would know more often when a piece is good. I think, in other words, we really have to *feel* an article is good and its subject is what we want to write about.

I remember a time six or seven years ago when I was out of assignments and had one of those three-month dry spells. I finally called *Reader's Digest* and in desperation said to an editor, "Is there anything in the shop you would like me to do?"

He dug around and probably got to the bottom of the barrel, called me and said, "We've a great subject for you. We want you to do a piece on mercury."

I said, "I haven't written much on astronomy."

He said, "No, the metal; all about mercury."

I said, "Oh. Great. It sounds fascinating."

I went to Washington, spoke to people in New York and learned a lot about mercury. After a while I thought this was a pretty interesting thing. But some part of me should have told me it wasn't my meat. To get to the snapper, it was rejected by the *Digest* and I later sold it to a minor science magazine. I hope I learned a lesson.

On the other hand, I once wrote a long, difficult piece on the Bell Telephone Laboratories; about people who are long-range planners for Bell, the men who try to predict fifteen to twenty years in advance what the System will need. This was for *Life.* When I turned that piece in, I knew it was good and I knew that everybody would be interested. But the editors of *Life* said, "Here is half your fee; please take it back along with our apologies. We think it is terribly technical and people won't really be interested."

I sent that piece around town and got the same answer from different editors, but I was convinced they were all wrong. Finally the piece wound up being accepted by *Fortune,* which almost never buys outside material. It was subsequently condensed by *Reader's Digest.*

I always believed this article was good but I never felt that way about the mercury piece. I really didn't *believe* it was good. Once it had been rejected, I knew I had been kidding myself.

How do I know when writing is really rewarding? I think it is when I get up early in the morning because I want to get to the desk or I want to get to the library when I am truly excited about what

I'm writing or researching. That, to me, is the real reward of being in this business. But there have been times, while working on pieces, when I actually hated going up the steps to my office to begin the day's work.

I have collected a number of danger signals for myself. There have been times when I found myself falling asleep over my own notes or typewriter. It's never really weariness. If I am bored by the article I am writing, even though I *think* I am not bored, sleepiness sets in.

There is another danger signal. Just when I start typing something I don't really like, I think, "Gee, I've got to call Murray. There's something I meant to ask him." Sometimes I'll go through three or four phone calls before my conscience says, "Knock it off, Buster; you are avoiding writing."

Running errands is yet another clue. When you suddenly realize you need another pair of shoes and you knock off early to get them; when you've heard that Harry Harris makes better shirts than anybody and you've been meaning to try Harry Harris for years and today is the day, that is another danger signal.

Conversely, when I love what I am doing, when I'm really engaged with it, I turn off my bell and give the order, "Answer the phone if it rings, but don't buzz me unless it's really important."

Finally, people say one of the troubles with the free-lance writer is that no matter what subject is brought up in the course of an evening, this guy has just written an article about it and will tell you all about it. But that is the safety signal. I consider it a danger signal when I am working on something I don't want to tell anybody about; when I don't feel full of it and flowing over; when I don't feel like bubbling with excitement about my present project.

—Morton Hunt

Break a Big Job into Small Pieces

If you feel overwhelmed by the enormity of a task, such as major revision of a long magazine piece or book, attack it calmly, in small understandable sections. Then, when you've completed work on them, take the long view of the entire project. Often you'll find, after the smaller sections have been revised, that the whole piece miraculously falls into fresh new order.

Once when I was working on a major article for *The Saturday Evening Post*—a critique of the debut in America—I found myself swamped with the many facets of the piece. In my case this was especially disturbing since I usually write profiles having an obvious single thread. I organized the mass of material topically, then read through the different subjects until I hit upon one that I could "see" in completeness in my mind's eye, wrote it first, repeated the process over and again and finally fit the whole cumbersome thing into a package.   *—Beth Day*

In the Space Provided — The Useful "TK"

I don't suppose any two article writers attack their work in exactly the same way. There are those who amass every fact relevant to the subject (quite enough to write a book) before they type a word of text—and then laboriously sift through the material to extract what's necessary for the specific work in hand. Others write a small set amount each day, then prune and polish the next morning. Some start writing any old how, in the certain knowledge that by tearing up pages one and two they will find that they have at least gotten into the meat of the subject and page three becomes the start.

In the bad old days when I had too little work and plenty of time (the bad old days ended about yesterday) I, too, collected every available fact in the form of pamphlets, book extracts, clippings, photocopies, which I stored in huge yellow envelopes and then, when I could find no more sources, I would start to write. Often the subject had by that time gone stale on me (or rather the other way around) and it was a struggle to compose not only a lead but any sentence that was not trite and obvious and stuffed with journalese; and that is why I have gone over to the tk technique.

It is a matter of writing the skeleton of the article early in your researches, often before you've even assembled a quarter of your material, but essentially at a moment when you are full of wit, originality, and enthusiasm for the subject; and the draft must be completed in one sitting. It will not be anything recognizable as a Piece and is likely to be full of words like "phtoograph" and "propsect," but the point is that being done quickly it will have cohesive form—a beginning, a middle and an end—and a certain continuity.

There will be gaps, of course. The article is about interstellar travel and you're not quite sure how long a light-year is, so many facts will have to be temporarily omitted and the blank spots marked with the conventional symbol for "to come"—tk. It might look like this:

"At the present highest estimate of   tk   mph for possible speeds through space, it would take some   tk   years for space explorers to reach the nearest star, which is   tk   light-years, or   tk   miles away from the earth; thus   tk   generations of spacemen and spacewomen would live and die during the journey."

The missing data can be calculated or discovered and filled in during any odd moments when you are devoid of creative inspiration and merely wish routine work to do.

You haven't yet lined up an interview with a reputable astronaut, so you leave a huge gap—half a page or more—for that. But there's no reason why you shouldn't sketch out the kind of information you are looking for:

"Major   tk   tk, who in 19tk made   tk   orbits of the earth, said he saw no reason why larger capsules and more knowledge about food preservation should not make interstellar travel possible—'but not in my lifetime,' he added."

It is a matter of doing the research from the article, instead of vice versa. The back of the work is broken early in the job; thenceforward you know what you are looking for. The original draft can be altered and added to with slips of paper stapled at one end to the margins, and my own first draft soon flaps and flutters like the unfinished work of those clever artists who used to entertain theater queues with scissors and paper.

It is a method which suits me, personally; and in a rack beside my desk are four or five manuscripts indecipherable to anyone but me, to which I can add a fact, a sentence or a paragraph from time to time as they come to hand, "in the space provided," as form-filling officials say. It is enabling me to get through my work faster; whereas last year I completed 30 articles, this year ought to see me sending out, well, as many as   tk .   —*J. A. Maxtone Graham*

Chapter Nine

VERIFYING FOR ACCURACY

To Protect Yourself, Send Checking Copies of Manuscripts

It is much better to send out copies of an article to the persons involved for checking before publication and get their kicks in advance than to risk angry (and warranted) complaints to the editor after publication. The former is the way to build a reputation for accuracy with editors—and to give your readers the accuracy to which they are entitled.

We recall one case in which we wrote a piece bitterly attacking the American meat industry for failing to clean up the hazard of trichinosis in pork. Prior to publication, a copy went to the American Meat Institute. An irate answer came back, saying that the article was unjustified, the hazard a minor one and, besides, we had made two mistakes on page seven. We corrected the two mistakes, the article appeared and everybody was relatively happy.

In the past 20 years our husband-and-wife writing team has sent out a thousand advance checking copies of the 200 articles we have had published. In not a single case did we regret having followed this policy. In two or three cases out of the thousand, a recipient of a checking copy tried an "end run"—that is, he tried to block publication by appealing directly or indirectly to the magazine. In not a single case did he succeed. Editors get a sense of security from knowing an article has been thoroughly checked. I am sure we get risky, sensitive, controversial assignments in large part because editors know that our pieces will be checked in advance.

Obviously we don't accept all the changes suggested to us when we get the checking copies back. We just write our critics and assure them that however they may dislike the article in the form finally published, they can be confident it would have been even worse without their helpful comments. We have never once had this procedure backfire.

One incidental advantage is that the people we interview speak far more frankly when they know that they will see an advance copy. A second incidental advantage is that we often get additional verisimilitudinous details jotted on the margins of checking copies which significantly strengthen our articles. A third incidental advantage is that we are much more warmly welcomed when we come back to the same source for information on a second article, or a sixth.

But these are merely incidental. The chief reason we go to the trouble of sending out checking copies is that we owe that much concern for accuracy to the readers for whom we write and to the editors and publishers who pay us our livelihood.

—Ruth and Edward Brecher

Setting Deadlines for the Return of Checking Copies

As a medical writer having frequent contact with doctors, medical scientists and other very cautious sources, I don't find it unethical or objectionable, when the situation warrants, to check back with copy. However, there are inherent dangers unless you approach this properly. First, assure the source that you are as interested as he in accuracy of content—perhaps even more so since you, in your objective editorial way, have no axes to grind or use.

Second, when you agree to this, make clear that you are checking facts or quotes and only these—not your organization of the manuscript, your syntax, etc. Scientists sometimes show as much fascination for manipulating words as they do germs and chemicals, but they do so less successfully.

Third, if you are so reckless as to mail copy to a scientist or doctor for checking, be sure you set a deadline. I usually say, "Please send any corrections of fact or any comments to me by one week, as I am working on a tight deadline. If I do not hear from you by then, I will assume this is OK and that you have no comments." You'll hear.   *—Theodore Berland*

The Sanctity of the Direct Quote

Far too often I have seen paraphrases and even suppositions (he *could* have said that) in place of what the subject actually did say. Aside from the morality involved, this practice serves to cut off the subject as a possible source for other pieces. There is no reason why a direct quotation cannot be checked by phone. I'm not saying that a quote can't be condensed (for example, eliding repetitious or superfluous material between sentence three and sentence ten if the meaning isn't changed). But when that is done, the quote as it will appear should be read to the subject. My own practice is to check all long direct quotes.

The cry, "I've been misquoted," is a legitimate complaint more often than it should be. It ought not happen. And it's having occurred frequently in the past is one reason, incidentally, why some subjects are balky and hostile.   *—Nat Hentoff*

Working in a Difficult Anecdote

If he can prove the truth of an anecdote, the writer can usually use it, even if his source later denies it. This happened to me when I was writing an article on hotels and was told by letter of a freak accident that occurred during World War II in a San Francisco hotel. A drunken serviceman, I was told, wandered stark naked through an open door at midnight. Instead of walking into the bathroom he stepped into the utility closet, from which he plunged several floors down the laundry chute into a huge pile of soiled linen in the basement. The soft linen prevented serious injury and the man lay there moaning until some of the hotel help found and returned him to his room. The next morning when he awoke and was told what had happened, he fainted from sheer fright at the thought of his experience.

I wrote to the hotel publicity director who had sent me the story, asking for the serviceman's name, the date and other details. The reply was firm: "Your informant is no longer with the hotel, and you can understand that we don't want this kind of bad publicity getting into print." I used the anecdote anyway, introducing it with these quite accurate words: "The Mark Hopkins Hotel would like to forget the time when . . . "   *—Alden Todd*

Checking Back the As-told-to Story with the Subject

Since the as-told-to piece is written in first person and by-lined by the subject, the writer who does *not* check out the manuscript for accuracy runs a serious risk of such unhappy consequences as libel suits or irate, threatening letters to the editor who has every right to feel that the writer he has assigned can be relied on for veracity. Whatever gripes or grumbles the subject may have are far, far better dealt with before publication.

The nub of the matter is not *whether* to check back with the subject on the manuscript, but *how*. Here I have made certain laws for myself; my own extensive experience with as-told-to stories has given them the nature of commandments.

1. *Do not* send the manuscript to the subject for leisurely perusal, probably in the company of close relatives and friends who at once constitute themselves a board of censorship and review.

*D*o arrange for a meeting alone with your subject.- Permit him to read the manuscript in your presence only. The point of insisting on this person-to-person contact over the manuscript is in the interests of obtaining the subject's own reaction, unlarded by the gratuitous advice of others and uncolored by the second thoughts and misgivings which all subjects feel about the projected piece when it nears publication.

2. *Do not* stand on your pride of authorship and attempt to cow the subject into submission on all points.

Do invite honest and thoughtful suggestions and criticism and accept them graciously, making whatever outright changes or compromises which seem reasonable to you.

Your subject person should not be regarded as a foe. The as-told-to relationship, if it is to produce a depth story, must proceed from friendship and empathy right up to the finish line. In my own experience, this friendship and empathy have, far more often than not, continued for years after the piece was published. Remember that the content of the piece is, after all, out of the subject's experience; the stylizing and presentation are yours.   —*Terry Morris*

Send Checking Copies to Learn New Information

I am all for sending scientific pieces to the principals involved for checking. I don't think anybody is controlling us when we do that, providing the understanding is clear. When I do a piece with the help of some agency or a university or an individual professor, I am willing to say in the first place that I will accept technical corrections, but where viewpoint or interpretation or style is concerned, though I will listen to your comments, I reserve the right to handle the writing as I see fit. My sources like and find comfort in this. They feel that if I listen I will hear sweet reason.

There is a secondary gain in sending the article out for checking, even if I don't accept all the corrections. Sometimes another source, equally valid, will say, "No, it is not that way, but this way." Then I have learned something new about my field. I learned, for instance, on a piece I did recently, that people in the Family Service business like to talk about social casework; and they hate the word psychotherapy because they are afraid of running into trouble with the medical profession. But if you ask other people, they will tell you it is "psychotherapy."

I never would have known that if I hadn't listened to their special pitch. I am better able to write about the subject this time, the next time and for the future. I learn something when I listen to experts argue about what I have written.   —*Morton Hunt*

Chapter Ten

TAPE RECORDERS — COPIERS — CAMERAS

Writing with the Recorder

For years I was convinced that I could write only on a typewriter and scoffed at the tape recorder afficionados. Not long ago, however, I was confronted with an extremely tight deadline on several chapters for a book. The material for these chapters was contained in about 30 different research papers and textbooks. In desperation I spread the material out over several tables and chairs and then, with rented tape recorder, began "writing." Although the result was far from "finished" copy, it did enable me to deliver copy on time.

Moral: be flexible.   *—S. L. Englebardt*

Earning the Cost of a Photocopier on One Job

This applies to professionals only—writers who must make their time count in dollars and cents. A photocopying machine, expensive as one may be, can be a worthwhile investment. Often I borrow books and documents, promising to return them soon, even though I may need some of their contents over a long writing project. I simply copy the pages I need on my photocopying machine and send the book back.

At other times I want notes from a page or two of a book. I hate to tear a book apart and hate even more to copy notes. So I merely copy the page and underline the pertinent information. In the course of once doing an article on social welfare in which many important people were trying to hide lots of important data, a brave and admirably sneaky bureaucrat loaned me a confidential report containing almost everything I needed. He said he had to have it back in three days. That was the day I bought my photocopier. In less than a day I selected and copied more than 100 pages that were useful to me, returned the original and was saved almost a week of dreadfully dull notetaking—even if I had the week to take. The time saved on that job alone paid for most of my machine.

Anyone getting a photocopier should make sure he gets a kind that can copy from a bound book. Some can, some can't. For a writer, this feature is essential. Another feature which may be useful for offices is not worth the price for most writers: the ability of some machines to make many duplicates from a single original. Writers usually need just one copy or, at most, two or three.

—*Bernard Asbell*

Note-Taking with a Tape Recorder

Somewhere in the midst of erratum there arose the legend that the keenest writers conduct interviews without taking notes. I've known men who boasted of such idiocy. But I've known only one writer with a true photographic memory and his talents were freakish.

The trend is in the opposite direction. There seems to be no limit these days to the avalanche of electronic gimmickry and much of it is of surpassing value to the professional writer.

The basic tool for any writer who is involved in interviewing is the tape recorder. Many writers own two or more: a pocket-sized battery model for short interviews or for use as an electronic notebook; a somewhat larger one, usually, which can operate either on battery or from an electrical outlet, for extensive work at home or in libraries. For the writer, recorders can be as sound an investment as a typewriter.

The most formidable research project I've encountered was for the study of the 11 western states that Random House published under the title of *Westward Tilt*. This was contemporary history: a blend of journalism and sociology, somewhat in the John Gunther tradition. It undertook to tell the story of the largest migration in the history of the world—the one to the American West since World War II. Sociologists hadn't tackled it before because the subject wouldn't hold still enough to meet their demands for a scientific study; journalism had treated it only in a fragmentary fashion.

So I spent much of the two years driving about the West, armed with tape recorders and portable Thermofax. There were no sources for my book except interviews, observation and the morgues of newspapers in towns and cities throughout the West.

In perhaps 2,000 interviews I found no one who objected to speaking into a tape recorder microphone. Instead, quite frequently my use of the recorder seemed to evoke that extra ounce of concentration and articulation. I spent weeks playing back those tapes, gleaning nuggets of information and occasional quotes and providing myself with a kaleidoscopic review of the territory.

One of the virtues of my smallest recorder—one which I hadn't anticipated—was that I found myself talking into it as I drove or as I dressed in the morning. This gave me a reservoir of an almost subconscious stream of thought which otherwise would have escaped; it also helped me to recapture settings and moods for descriptive passages of the book which resulted.

I suspect that most writers say things to themselves which mean a great deal more than some of the things they set down on paper. Therefore, since I learned my lesson, I am seldom far from a pocket-sized recorder into which I may confide. Talking vague ideas out on tape can help firm them into salable material.

My recorder and I first became inseparable during a rugged backroad drive in the foothills of Idaho's Sawtooth Range. I was en route to Sun Valley and a service station attendant tried to discourage me from taking my proposed road.

"I wouldn't ride over it in a Jeep," he said. "Three cars came in here this week off that road and they were all shaken apart."

I remember talking his words into my tape recorder a moment later as I obstinately turned to follow the backroad and, in the desolate splendor of the miles ahead, I kept talking to the little microphone at my side. Some of the tape went into the book just as I talked it then and I know it would have been impossible for me later to recapture detail like this:

> *The asphalt ended and a narrow ribbon of dirt wound off through glens of willow and alder and cottonwood and Rocky Mountain ash, past herds of sheep. Houses fell behind. In a ravine at the turn of a hairpin curve, a sheepherder's wagon stood beneath a great lodgepole pine, his stovepipe extending through the roof of the wagon. Ahead and above were mountainsides dense with fir and cedar and pine. At a mountain crossroads called Dixie stood a two-story frame house, deserted, its windows cracked and open. A house trailer took its place nearby, and a faded wooden sign pointed down an even more tenuous lane to hamlets named Pine and Atlanta. Then the road soared through green valleys and curved through forests like a roller coaster. A blue lake shimmered in the distance. Here and there a weathered, abandoned farmhouse, its roof collapsed, subsided into the landscape. There were no cars but mine. I had forgotten the joy of driving a lonely backroad where a man has a choice to drive on the left side of the road if it beckons, or in the middle if he is so inclined, without single lines, double lines, broken lines, passing lines, or center islands. Hawks flew up in the road ahead, and a great bald eagle soared from a cliffside nearby. The road led over Wild Horse Creek. At a sudden ninety-degree turn, I saw my trail of dust for miles behind.*

Besides, when I take notes I have trouble reading them.

—*Neil Morgan*

Copy Machine — A "Writing" Essential

Personally, I rank the copy machine third among writing essentials, right after my typewriter and dictating machine. Some writers might disagree. They might rank the copy machine fourth—after the tape recorder.

My copy machine—a portable "dry" copy lightweight type— more than returned its original price the first week I had it. And it has been daily proving itself indispensable ever since.

But that first week illustrates how valuable—really, how invaluable—the right kind of copy machine can be to a writer.

I'd been assigned a major crime story by a major men's magazine. That meant digging into the police files. But the files in question (at police headquarters) were, first of all, not open to "digging" (by writers, at any rate) and removing them from the police department was against the rules, too. Then, in an interview with the police captain who had charge of the files, I mentioned—not by accident but by design—that I just happened to have a portable copy machine in the car.

He winked . . . and we made a deal. He put the stack of files on his desk, told me he was going to leave his office for two hours and locked me in (with the files and my copy machine). Needless to say, by the time he returned I'd copied the entire police file on my portable copy machine. We shook hands and I left with a complete copy (more than 100 pages) of the police dossier in my briefcase. Without my portable copier and the research time it saved me, I doubt I'd been able to complete the assignment.

Actually, the portable model wasn't the first copy machine I'd owned. Back ten years ago I bought one of the very first "dry" copiers then on the market. That standard, desk-bound machine also made copies without use of liquid chemicals. The chemical-type copiers aren't practicable for most writers. First, chemicals are unhandy and expensive. Secondly, the chemical machines can't be carried with you, since you risk spilling their fluids. And, because they're ordinarily quite heavy, weight alone rules them out when you're on a quick fly-in assignment—when you've got to travel light or else pay for the extra weight.

Finally, a dry portable machine can go anywhere with you—even

to the Arctic (as I have) in the dead of winter. Up there, at
—50° F., chemicals freeze. A dry-type copy machine copies what
you need to copy, anywhere; in a police captain's office . . . or in
subzero weather.   *—James Joseph*

Taking Notes from Your Own Taped Interviews

On no more than a half dozen occasions in the past ten years have
I ever used a tape recorder for getting down an interview. Like most
reporters, I usually find a little notebook adequate—in fact, preferable. But sometimes you run into someone who talks fast or with
such depth or with so personal a flavor of speech that note-taking
would cause great loss of what the interviewee is saying.

This brings up two old problems. First, doesn't the presence of
a machine inhibit the talker? I have found that it may do so for the
first five or ten minutes, but if the reporter succeeds in getting his
interviewee deeply engaged in the subject, which is the aim of any
good interview, he rapidly forgets the machine is there. The second
problem often raised is that transcribing the material of the tape
can be lengthy, expensive and largely wasteful. That problem is
easily solved. Instead of transcribing the tape, all the writer need
do is listen to a playback and in his own leisurely way jot down
notes on what he wants (pressing the button to stop the machine
while he does so) and ignoring the rest. It's a great advantage.
Wouldn't it be marvelous to be able to press a button on a live
interviewee to start and stop him while you took notes—and yet not
goof up his thinking processes?   *—Bernard Asbell*

Collecting Vivid Detail with a Camera

Few magazine writers, not even those compulsive researchers who
fill several spiral steno pads when they're off on an assignment, ever
feel that they have accumulated all the detailed research material
they need once they sit down to start writing the article. Almost
everyone realizes, too late, that they've forgotten some trivial but
fascinating detail—the shape of a subject's head, the appearance

of a certain street, the exact lines of a particular building vital to the article.

Like most writers, I seldom have a second chance if I forget to make careful notes of such detail. I may research an article in Scotland or the Dominican Republic, Vienna or Timbuktu and then come back to New York to review the notes and commence the business of writing.

But for 12 years now I've owned a Minox camera, small enough to fit into my pocket, easy to operate, 50 pictures per roll of film, around $120 (at least at the time I bought mine) and, happy day, a legitimate and deductible business expense. Whenever I'm off on an assignment I snap pictures—nothing artistic, just pictures of the people I interview, buildings, vegetation, landmarks, the works.

In my apartment, often half a world away from where I did my research, I start writing the article with a set of these pictures thumbtacked to a wallboard over my desk. If I want to know **exactly** what the farmhouse looked like outside Vienna, where the spy ring trained its field agents, all I do is look at the set of photographs.

In doing an article for the now defunct *American Weekly,* for example, about an East German who had been intimidated by the Communist espionage apparatus to gather material from American servicemen in Berlin, I referred several times to close-ups I had taken of the girl in a West Berlin prison where I conducted the interviews. I had a fairly good memory of what she looked like, since I had interviewed her only the month before, but I had less recollection of the interior of the prison, her cell and even a couple of features (full eyes, snub nose) of the girl herself—the last of which were pertinent because her wonderfully good looks were what gave her access to American soldiers. The point here is that I could line the article with detail, vivid, close-up detail, with those pictures spread before me as I worked.

For a writer in search of the detail that helps bring an article to life, a Minox camera the size of a cigarette lighter is no longer a luxury item. It's downright essential.   —*Robert G. Deindorfer*

Book Writing with a Tape Recorder

During the past ten years I've turned out twelve books and at least 100 magazine articles and not one was "written" per se—each was, rather, dictated. I believe a recording machine of some kind to be indispensable to the full time professional writer. When I went to the Caribbean to write two books a couple of years ago, I left my typewriter at home and took my dictating machine.

My first electronic device was a tape recorder which I got more as a hobby than anything else. I looked with disfavor upon the idea of dictating stories; I didn't think it would be possible to transmit depth of feeling and expression in this new-fangled fashion. Shortly after finishing research for a book, however, I suffered a recurrence of a war injury and found myself confined to a supine position with my tape recorder. I therefore "wrote" the book by speaking into a microphone on my chest, manipulating a foot-pedal resting on my stomach. It was exceedingly difficult for me at first, adjusting to this new medium, but there was little choice. I realize now that I was fortunate; the transition from typing to dictating might have floored me, as it has many other writers, if I'd been able to choose.

Since then I have produced prodigious amounts of copy in short periods of time. I recall once turning out a 15,000-word book-length article in 48 hours. It was dictated, typed, revised and retyped and it wasn't bad. This sort of thing only pays the usual article rates and if you spend weeks on it, you're dead. If you can get it out fast, it's profitable.

I have over a thousand dollars' worth of recording equipment and it has paid for itself many times. First in the order of usage on a job comes the battery-powered portable tape recorder. Good ones list for about a hundred bucks up. Then comes a larger machine with a foot pedal attachment and earphones for the typist to use when transcribing the tapes. You may not need both of these machines. For dictating copy, I don't recommend either one. A standard office dictating machine is greatly superior. My own choice is a Stenocord, which I prefer far and away to any other, for several reasons.

Most people think first of recording interviews. For short interviews, I'm not too high on recorders. It usually takes a few minutes for the subject to become at ease with a mike—some people much longer. Some orate; they *on mike!* You've then got all that dead stuff recorded and you either have to listen to it yourself or have it typed, both of which consume time and take away your zest for the story. For the one-shot interview of an hour or less, 99 times out of 100 pen and paper work best.

Occasionally I interview someone—usually an important figure —who appreciates being recorded and I get better results even on a short interview with a tape recorder. Lawyers and politicians, for example, are impressed when you plug in, hook up, test and then put the mike in front of them. They're always on stage anyway, at least in their own minds. Once I was having a great deal of trouble pinning down an eccentric genius for whom I was supposed to ghost a book. I tracked him to his summer retreat where he was lying by his pool in a beach chaise, rigged up a pole to which I could hang the microphone directly over his face and began. When I started the tape recorder he was intrigued, almost entranced, and from then on he looked forward to our interviews.

Even when a tape recorder is not used for interviewing, it can come in handy afterwards. In one hectic month a few years ago, while researching two books, I traveled from coast to coast and from Michigan to Florida interviewing people. I must have talked to 300 people in 50 communities. Frequently there'd be several people at lunch or dinner, all talking, and I couldn't take notes, much less run a tape recorder. At the end of each day, however, I'd sit down and dictate all I had learned during the day, plus the descriptions of people and their relevant quotes. In this manner I could clear my mind of cluttering details and be pleasantly ready for the next day. On this trip, incidentally, I did not use a tape recorder, but the Stenocord which records on a magnetic sleeve. I'd ship the small sleeves home to my wife in an ordinary 5 x 7-inch envelope and she'd transcribe the material and return the sleeves to me at my next stop. Anything else would have been cumbersome and expensive.

A recorded interview is just like any other interview. You can't just turn on the machine and go to sleep. You've got to keep alert, keep prodding and prying and poking. I constantly make notes during an interview of things to bring up later. This feature alone is worth the price of the equipment. You don't have to interrupt your man to get details of a point or explore an intriguing tangential matter. Just make a note for future reference and let him go on.

Incidentally, do not expect your interview to come out of the tape recorder as sparkling and scintillating as it went in. When a person talks he gesticulates, gives you meaningful looks, smiles and frowns and emphasizes his points with vocal inflections. The transcription of this interview has none of these furbishments, just little black marks on yellow paper. It's flat. I do not hesitate to take liberties with the words of my subjects, rearranging them, adding and cutting, in order to make my people read on paper the way they sound on tape. Nobody has ever objected.

This is one reason why I don't show my transcripts to my subjects. I don't think I have any obligation to do so unless it was so specified before the tape started to roll . . . and only once has this occurred. I have never recorded an interview without the subject's knowledge, incidentally, and I don't think I ever will.

When the research is done and it's time to go to work, I usually take the transcript and, using scissors and Scotch tape, chop it up and organize it. (People don't like to be interrupted and told to stick to the subject. Let 'em ramble.) Paradoxically, although I am advocating use of recording devices here, I usually like to write the first paragraph, page or pages on the typewriter. I feel I'm getting more warmth into it. When I get going, I shift to the microphone. I'm pretty explicit. I say what the story is, say "paragraph," spell out proper nouns and specify each punctuation mark. When my daughter Sue was a toddler, she once asked her mother who that girl was I was talking to, that girl named "Comma."

I find that when I dictate I talk too much, a trait which comes as no big surprise to many. Redundancy is the curse of the big mouth. Nor is my dictation light and bright; cleverness apparently is something you have to see on the paper in front of you. However, the verbosity can always be cut away and the light touches dovetailed in. Frankly, regardless of whether I dictate the first draft or write it, I'm going to revise to some degree. The misery in writing as far as I'm concerned is getting something on paper. I can get it there quicker and easier by mouth. I recommend the method to you.

—*Booton Herndon*

Photography for Writers

A camera can be a highly valuable tool in researching, organizing and even selling a story. For example, I have filmed documents, letters and other printed material, all of which are permanently available for reference later on. My camera often can substitutte for a notebook.

Pictures of people, places and situations help to refresh a writer's memory when he's working on a story. And the longer the interval between first researching and actual writing, the more valuable such pictures become.

Frequently an outline-plus-photos will sell a story to an editor where an outline alone will not. One good example is a story of strip coal mining that I finished recently. The editor could not conceive the complete and vast destruction of strip mining to a formerly beautiful landscape in eastern Ohio. Nor could he see the desolation it left behind. But a series of photos along with the query were convincing enough and these led to a 3200-word piece, "America's Real Red Menace," in *Sports Afield*.

And sometimes truly good photographs, good enough to be used as illustrations, will inspire or justify stories which otherwise would never be written.   —*Erwin A. Bauer*

Backing Up Your Memory wtih Tape

It may be marginally illegal, but keep your telephone bugged so that you can record interviews on tape. Even if you never play back the tape as you write, relying only on your notes, it's reassuring to have the tape to fall back upon when and if a source later claims he was misquoted. Another tip: if you use a transistorized recorder, turn off any nearby fluorescent lights, as they generate much noise. You can buy little telephone pick-up attachments cheaply. They attach by suction cups. Move the instrument around to see where the best pick-up is. —*Theodore Berland*

The Subminiature Camera Helps a Writer in Many Ways

I find it advantageous to take along a good subminiature camera on assignments. When loaded with a fast fine-grain film, it permits the writer to "shoot" scenes, objects and people unobtrusively and in natural light. This can be helpful in a number of ways.

For one thing, there is often a long time lapse between gathering the material and putting it down on paper in finished form. A photographic record of faces and places aids the recall of details that belong in the story.

Here is a case in point. I recently completed an assignment for a story on severely disturbed children. There were many people to see and their time was limited. I photographed them instead of writing down their physical descriptions. I took candid shots of the teachers at work with the children, posed close-ups where permission to do so was granted and snapped shots of the unusual setting. I also copied the children's lesson papers, drawings and doodlings. As it turned out, I was unable to write the article directly after finishing my research; another sudden assignment intervened. Fortunately, my picture record bridged the gap when eventually I sat down to write the article.

Also, a collection of revealing photographs may be of assistance to an editor in guiding him on how to illustrate the article. In fact, some shots may be good enough for reproduction purposes.

A side benefit is worth mentioning. Interviewees will usually be delighted to receive copies of the photographs (provided they are flattering) and will warmly remember the writer upon his next visit.

The subminiature is extremely useful as a copying tool. Since it enables photographs to be taken from close distances, it offers a quick, inexpensive means of recording documents of all kinds. An accessory flash attachment of minute size makes the recording of written material foolproof.   —*Arthur Henley*

Using a Foot Pedal to Edit Tape Interviews

Most writers who use tape recorders for interviews find that they record a great deal of material which, although interesting, is largely irrelevant to the subject of the article. And, of course, many interviewees digress with boring dissertations or asides which the writer knows he will not use in the finished piece. To turn off the tape recorder on these occasions would be distracting to the interviewees and give him the impression that you don't consider what he is saying as being worthwhile. However, there is a way of turning off the tape recorder without the interviewees being too aware of it. It is through the use of a foot pedal, a device available for most tape recorders. The foot pedal is also used later when transcribing the tape at your typewriter.   —*Carl Bakal*

Dictating an Article Point by Point

Not only do I dictate notes, but I often dictate articles as well. Here's how I proceed. First I dictate a note to myself embracing highlights of my research in one-two-three order. In one food story, for example, I wanted to make the reader aware that many super-markets and groceries are bilking consumers with little sums that add up to millions yearly. I also wanted readers to know how to avoid being thus taken, by being charged for items not put into their grocery bags, getting second quality and so forth. And, at the same time, I wished to make it quite clear that most food sellers are basically honest.

By dictating points off, each in a separate paragraph, I find that on first drafts I am not too concerned with *how* I am saying it. Rather, I get down the essentials of *what* I want to say. With this story, and with others, I may very well rearrange my point order as soon as I see the typed draft. But by using my list as a basic guide, I know that as I get each point dictated into the story and cross it off, my piece begins to add up to what I want to convey to the reader.

Next, even if I have no specific idea of how the piece should begin, I start dictating with the best idea I possess at the moment. In the food story mentioned, I knew I wanted an anecdote that would instill reader identification. Not having one at the time I dictated a note to myself indicating how I wanted to open, then moved on to subsequent points. I make myself talk from one idea to the next to get the form of the piece, from which I can work further.

When I don't have the case or example I need, I simply dictate a reminder to that effect or the words "blank and blank" which my secretary indicates like this: ——— and ———. Then I go on. I've found that the missing matters over which I might have wasted anywhere from a few minutes to an hour, invariably come to me (often from later notes) as I move from draft to draft.

—Ray Josephs

Taking Written Notes while Tape Recording

Even while I am recording an interview, I always try to take a complete set of notes. This allows me to be reasonably fail-safe in case something goes wrong with my recorder and I've failed to turn the volume up enough or forgotten to put the handle on "record"— which I've done enough times to make me uncomfortable every time I conduct an important interview.

Another advantage in this is that if your interview turns out to be worthless except for one or two items, you can always discard the tape and simply use your notebook.

I always take notes in a spiral notebook, but sometimes it becomes inconvenient to carry an unwieldy notebook with you or make an unavoidable display of flipping it open. A solution to this problem is simply to carry a smaller notebook, one that can be carried inside a breast pocket. Or, instead of a small notebook, a dozen blank 3 x 5-inch cards may suffice.   —*Hal Higdon*

Using a Dictating Machine in the Library

A dictating machine is of great value in library research and at various official agencies and other places where you have to go through a mass of printed materials. Consider the Better Business Bureau, for example. Looking through their files for food gyps, as I did on one piece, and taking handwritten notes would have required hours of the most valuable commodity any writer has— his time. But I took my dictating machine along, read off everything that interested me, noting sources, and had the notes transcribed later. Your library will usually give you a quiet corner or small conference room for dictation. Three hours of dictating give me the equivalent of two days of hand note-taking. My dictation, however, is more accurate. Quotations I might have skipped because of weariness are recorded.   —*Ray Josephs*

Chapter Eleven

FILING

Saving Profiles from Time Magazine

Ever since I've been subscribing to *Time* I have been saving, from
each issue which features one, the profile cover story. I tear each
one out, staple the pages together and file. As a result, I have a
library of the world's leading personalities—a dossier containing a
wealth of information on contemporary VIPs. In these *Time* profiles,
which are pretty accurately researched, you've got the hobbies of
every notable, his religion, alma mater, number of children, even
the color of his eyes.

How can this file be helpful? I once suggested an article for
the Father's Day issue of *This Week,* "Will Your Son be a Chip off
the Old Block?" In other words, if you were a doctor, would your
son be a physician? If you were a farmer, would your son follow
in your footsteps? To give my piece verisimilitude, I thought it
would be appropriate to discuss the fathers of contemporary sons
and their professions. Consulting my *Time* "morgue," I discovered
that Bernard Baruch's father was a physician; Liberace's pa was an
undertaker; Dale Carnegie's dad was a farmer; Cecil B. DeMille's
father was a lay preacher, and so on. Needless to say, this impressive
"name-dropping" helped me sell my article as a lead piece.

—Mort Weisinger

Filing Names of Sources and Story Ideas

While every professional writer should have a dictionary and thesaurus at his elbow for ready reference, it is also a valuable aid to maintain an alphabetical card file listing the names of sources for different types of information.

These sources can include everything from the names, addresses and telephone numbers of specialized libraries to the same information about public relations people who handle specific companies.

For example, I write a lot in the aerospace field. I know the topic quite well. I know which companies are building various parts of the spacecraft. Under the heading of these companies—their names—I have the names of the public relations men I deal with and their office and home telephone numbers and addresses. If, for instance, I have had occasion to interview a top engineer or scientist working for this company, I will also have his telephone extension and make arrangements to phone him in the future. In this way I can avoid going through public relations and can phone my man directly. On the other hand, I always advise the PR contact that I have spoken to one of the company's technical personnel. This courtesy is appreciated in many ways—by the PR man and by the subject of the interview, who knows that his company PR office will become aware of the conversation.

Sources and source materials are built up over a period of time and the professional writer builds his files with experience.

I, for one, know that I'm likely to write in the future about life under the sea—man's existence beneath the sea. I therefore purchase a few basic books on the subject and read them in my spare time. When a story idea about life beneath the sea comes through in the form of a news clipping, I can pitch an idea to a magazine based on more than the knowledge from the clipping.

An editor is then inclined to feel, considering my detailed outline, that I know my subject. For, invariably, an editor has read the same story and clipped it as a story possibility, too. —*Edward Hymoff*

Careful Background Files Reduce the Need for Legwork

The limitations that a full-time job place on the ability of the spare-time freelance writer to do the necessary legwork for an article, can often be circumvented by a rather simple device—the background file. Many of my articles and three of my books were written out of my background files without additional research, interviews or field trips.

In my files I have background materials on at least 50 subjects in my field of special interest, which happens to be health and medicine. To keep abreast of developments in medicine, I regularly scan medical journals and other professional publications. Whenever I come across a reference, a discussion, a report or a scientific paper on one of my pet subjects, I clip the material and toss it into the proper background folder. I also scan the programs of important professional meetings to see if papers are being delivered on subjects of interest to me.

If a reference in a publication or a program is too skimpy to be useful, I write to the scientist or the physician referred to for a copy of his paper, a fuller report or personal comments. Often the individual responds and supplies me with far more materials—previously published papers, for example—than I had requested. Additional materials on a subject may also be available from professional societies or other interested groups. The American Academy of Pediatrics or the American Association of Blood Banks, for example, supply information from their special fields of interest. Quite regularly, health agencies such as the American Heart Association or The Arthritis Foundation are eager to help.

In time, each background folder grows and, periodically, I go through the folders to check whether I have accumulated enough background material on one subject to permit me to suggest an article idea to an editor. It is amazing how often a folder will contain everything that I need to write an article, including notes, anecdotes, statistics and other details. If my material seems somewhat dated, a few letters to some of the people named in the material on file will bring things up to date. Sometimes a news item will suggest the idea for an article, thus providing the new lead for the remainder, which will come out of my background files.   —*William Kitay*

Keeping in Touch with Your Best Sources

Here is a technique that might be useful to anyone specializing in a particular area or special subject. For over six years I covered Alaska and Canada for *Reader's Digest*. Over that time I met hundreds of people who were immediately or potentially useful as sources of information. I have since endeavored to keep track of all of them, maintaining—as much as possible—an up-to-date 3 x 5-inch index card file, including name, address, telephone number, area of interest and last contact. On dull days I may write to two or three of these sources, sociably, and invariably receive a bonus of new information from, say, Nome, Inuvik or Halifax. And, in a pinch, I find myself with a system of stringers all across the North Country, every bit as willing as *Time's*.   —*Lawrence Elliott*

Read and Clip Newspapers Systematically

Writers dealing with subjects likely to be affected by the news must read the papers. You can save a lot of time in doing so if you do it in a planned and purposeful way—in a single reading, looking at all the headlines, tearing out at once and dating every story that you think will interest you. Take the attitude expressed by Julius Caesar in Shaw's "Cleopatra," in that you pass this way but once. Much time can be wasted trying to locate something you saw in the Sunday paper and intended—but neglected—to clip. You can find many ideas for articles in newspapers, but try to cover some besides the *New York Times*—everybody sees that one. *The Boston Globe, Christian Science Monitor, Detroit Free Press, Detroit News, Milwaukee Journal, Kansas City Star, Washington Post, Denver Post, Los Angeles Times* and *Miami Herald* often have magazine caliber material.   —*Tom Mahoney*

Use a Metal-edged Ruler for Clipping

It's time-consuming and awkward to clip newspapers and magazine articles with a scissors. I do the job quickly with an 18-inch metal ruler. I've learned that it's efficient to accumulate about a week's worth of clippings in a file basket on my desk. Then I spread the newspapers out on a large work table (dining room table is fine) and tear each item along the edge of the ruler. To complete the job, I date my clips at the head with a rubber stamp before filing.

—Marvin Weisbord

Clipping Items of General Interest to Build Files

I do a great deal of general research so that when an article is to be started on any of the major subjects which interest me—women, men and women, religion, civil rights, the lost creativity or joy in people —there is already on hand a good deal of material. I subscribe to such publications as the *Journal of the American Association of University Women; Marriage and Family Living;* the publications of the National Council of Churches and others, as well as general magazines and newspapers.

I clip for this pile about fifteen minutes a day. The clippings pile up until there is a box or suitcase full of them and then they are sorted into big manila envelopes labeled with specific headings. I wish I had the temperament for a really good filing system, but I don't—and this seems to work pretty well.   *—Ardis Whitman*

Keeping Track of Sources

Each time I use a book or magazine article, I make a 3 x 5-inch card for my permanent file. This card, filed by author's last name, lists the name of the book or article, date, publisher, sub-title and other pertinent data. To this I add the library call number, plus identifying letters to tell me which library has the book (i.e., FL means Free Library of Philadelphia; HC is Haverford College Library; UP is University of Pennsylvania Library). Finally, I make

a note or two of the book's value to me. This last is important.
You can go back again and again over the years to a book with a
provocative title if you forget that the contents are worthless. It
pays to keep a permanent record of what you consider good and
bad books.

Here is a sample card:

Hasseltine, William B.   FL.

                                                            B
ULYSSES S. GRANT, POLITICIAN   G—76428
(N.Y. DODD, MEADE & CO. 1935)

Good, Sympathetic bio of Grant with much detail
and many quotes from original documents.

Taking notes from books or articles, I use a 5 x 8-inch notecard.
At the top goes only the author's name and a few words of reference to my permanent bibliography card. For example, a note
taken from the book mentioned above would be headed thus:

Hasseltine, Grant, p. 18

I don't have to write out the full reference each time. I can
always get it from my permanent file.   —*Marvin Weisbord*

Filing Data on "Big" Names

Writing chronically, as I do, about various diseases and how they threaten us, how we're closing in on them and allied points, I have used a successful ploy that adds reader interest. Ulcers become a little more interesting when the reader knows that a famous senator suffered from one; bronchiectasis, now a famous lung disorder, is more meaningful when we are told that the late President Johnson suffered from it; and when we speak of pneumonia, it is more likely to catch our eye when we learned that actor William Bendix died of it.

So, while at first it appears ghoulish, I read the obituaries and sickness write-ups. I particularly look for the deaths and illnesses of prominent people, then file their obits or clips under my cheery diseases reference files.   *—Theodore Berland*

Chapter Twelve

WRITING AS A BUSINESS

Tips for Writing Overseas

To writers considering living and writing overseas, here are some tips from one who spent two years working out of Hong Kong:

1. Choose an area—Western Europe, Japan, Southeast Asia, the Caribbean—likely to be of interest to many American magazines. Avoid such areas as the Pacific Islands, India, the Near East, which are likely to provide you with few salable pieces in a year.

2. Set up deals with leading magazines, if possible. Even staff written books like *Newsweek* or *U.S. News* are often willing to set up stringer arrangements with free-lancers going to unmanned spots. Arrange a series of meetings with likely editors. Try to get yourself identified in their minds as "their man" in Switzerland, Rome, Beirut, etc.

3. Try to get Department of Defense accreditation in Washington. This means filling out forms and getting a magazine to swear you are "on their staff full time," but a small amount of negotiation in this area often can be completed with a compliant editor. Your card, if you get it, often can get you courtesy press transportation to and from critical areas when flashed in front of Air Force officers.

4. Contact radio and TV people in advance. Although you're a writer, if you know how to work a tape recorder you can be quite valuable to a network or station. The "talk" shows such as "Monitor" often use short tapes about exotic customs and habits overseas.

5. Get to know the local journalists overseas and make yourself available for local writing assignments. The USIA (United States Information Agency), for example, always needs help. Perhaps you can back up the bureau chiefs of the American news magazines or wire services, too. Bob McCabe came to Hong Kong with a few tenuous free-lance assignments. Soon he was backing up Bob Elegant in the *Newsweek* bureau. When Elegant left suddenly, McCabe was elevated to bureau chief because it was uneconomical for *Newsweek* to send a new man all the way out when a competent man was already there.

6. If your overseas base city has an English language newspaper, approach them with the idea of doing a travel column. I did this in Hong Kong, receiving the princely sum of $25 a week for 3,000 words. But I also earned about $6,000 worth of airplane tickets from PR people in one year and flew several times to Europe and throughout Asia on assignment as a result of my column.

7. When sending copy to the U.S., always use Airmail and register your manuscripts to insure safety. Ask your editors to reply by Airmail, too. It may take six weeks to receive a rejection otherwise.

8. Keep carbons of everything you do and negatives of all pictures. Don't ever let the "last" copy of anything leave your hands.

9. Get a Post Office Box where you live so that even when you move about locally you have one fixed address at which to receive mail. Hire a local steno to open your box and read your mail. She can deposit checks or wire you (you've given her your itinerary) should something come up while you're on the road.

—*Arturo F. Gonzalez, Jr.*

Put a Work Table in Your Office

One of the more useful pieces of furniture in my office is the large work table. For many jobs it is more convenient than my desk. This table is six feet long by thirty inches wide. (A picnic table with plywood top and a few coats of varnish works nicely).

On many of my assignments I must work with photographs. The work table, which is equipped with a viewer, is an excellent place for this work. It is also a good place to lay out book materials when organizing chapters. There are also times when a writer works on more than one article at once and such a work table gives him ample room to sort his materials without getting projects mixed up.

—*George Laycock*

How to Work with Researchers

Some writers use editorial researchers regularly, while others seem to feel that this is some form of cheating, like hiring someone to help a student write his term paper. Good researchers, however, are almost essential to any major writing project. A writer who is preparing a profile of a personality obviously has to spend a great deal of time with the subject in order to evaluate him and write about him. It lends depth to the writing, however, to use qualified researchers to conduct interviews, either with the subject or with persons who know him.

In other types of writing, researchers not only can do a good part of the legwork, but can readily provide different viewpoints on a subject, thus adding depth to the writer's concept. Sometimes I have picked researchers deliberately because their views on a subject conflicted with mine, or used female researchers in order to get the woman's outlook.

Another use for the writer-researcher type is in gathering technical or highly specialized material. A writer can waste a good deal of time unnecessarily on a project by trying to ferret out, decipher and write clearly about specialized information which a researcher knowledgeable in that field might be able to put together in a jiffy.

The extent to which a writer uses researchers has to be based on the income he expects from an assignment, the tightness of the deadline and the extent to which he values his own time. A good library researcher charges about $6-$10 an hour. A graduate student

—often qualified for this kind of work—might charge $4. Research-
ers experienced in general reporting and interviewing might range
from $6-$10 an hour. Some go as high as $15, but only in special
cases or when bringing the assignment some special knowledge of
the subject which is, in itself, of extra value.

The cost-per-hour goes down, in most cases, where a researcher
is assigned by the day or week. Thus, a $6 per hour researcher
might have a daily rate of only $40 and a weekly rate of $190. It
depends, too, upon the geographical locations. Researchers in large
cities come much higher than those in small towns. Researchers
abroad in some locations work at ridiculously low rates. A stringer
in Spain, for example, who was himself an experienced newspaper
editor and author of books, once charged me only $55 for a full
week's work—but that was quite some time ago.

How does a writer go about lining up researchers, especially
where he has no contacts initially? The most reliable source I know
is the managing editor or city editor of the local newspaper. Simply
write him a letter introducing yourself, describing yourself, describing
your own qualifications (an author's bio sheet is appropriate), and
telling him briefly the nature of the assignment. Do not go into
detail about the work, but simply ask him to recommend a qualified
person who does freelance researching or reporting. The chances
are, if you have used the professional approach, you will receive
an answer.

Other sources are: managing editors of local magazines; the
editors in charge of branch offices of national and international
magazines (such as *Time, Reader's Digest* or *Look);* book publishers; other writers. Libraries and colleges also can recommend researchers, but usually only of the kind qualified for reference work.

—*Wilbur Cross*

Tax Tips for Freelancers
Most writers don't deduct enough for legitimate expenses. Mainly
this costly oversight stems from the fact that many freelancers are
not used to thinking of themselves as independent entrepreneurs,

a special kind of business person marketing a highly individualized kind of product. Everything that enters into the conception of the idea, the preparation of the selling outline, the research of the article and final selling, involves deductible items. The obvious ones—the daily newspaper, magazine subscriptions, book purchases—are probably included in most freelancers' deductions, but there are some others less obvious.

Are you deducting *enough* for the professional use of your home or apartment? You are entitled to deduct a portion (if you have six rooms, the portion is one-sixth) of your mortgage or rent, phone bill, gas and electric bill (see the specific IRS rules on this), water bill, your car, your car insurance, your furniture (you can "sell" your own furniture to yourself if you're opening an office), and portions of certain kinds of home repairs, such as a new roof.

Are you deducting enough for unreimbursed travel expenses? Are you deducting enough for every trip, whether or not the magazine compensates you? Many of the items don't come with paid receipts: taxis, phone calls, tips.

Get yourself a Diners' Club or American Express card. Besides providing a detailed record of many of your entertainment and business expenditures, the cards have another useful function: they can save you money. For example, if you use the card to bill your airline ticket—domestic or foreign—you get the continued use of the money in your checking account for at least another month . . . before you get billed.

Can you deduct your spouse's expenses when accompanying you on a magazine assignment in California or Europe or Mexico? You can if you've been careful to establish your spouse as a bona fide (a) researcher or (b) co-author. There needn't be a joint byline every time. One every few years should be enough. But don't describe your spouse as your secretary: this is the unimaginative gambit some business people use. Since most writers have used or still use their spouses for part-time research work, taking a deduction is not only truthful but provable.

The income-averaging law is now there to provide the whipped cream when you have a particularly good year or your book is selling well. As long as your income jumps more than a third over the previous year, you can use this new provision to make considerable savings in your income tax.

If you carry one of the annual air travel insurance policies—Airways Club, for example—be sure to transfer *ownership* of the policy to your spouse. In the event of your death in an air accident, the proceeds of the policy would be considered part of your estate and thus taxable—but not if the policy was previously assigned to your spouse. Make sure that over the years you collect a portion of the overall cost of your annual air travel policy each time you bill a magazine for expenses incurred in traveling.

Don't do your income tax yourself. Get an accountant who handles other writers, if possible, or at least others self-employed. The cost will be recouped several times over in tax savings.

—*Murray Teigh Bloom*

Agree on Details In Advance

The way I have always worked—and I think most experienced free-lance writers do similarly—is to request a letter confirming the assignment, the price to be paid and the agreement on expenses. If I discover during the course of my research that my expenses will be going higher than planned, I telephone or write the editor for further clearance before proceeding. I do not expect the editor to pay expenses he has not approved.

It is your responsibility to deliver what you have promised. This means to deliver an article of the agreed-upon length, to deliver it on schedule, to deliver it in the form that your editor expects and can use.

Obviously, it must be absolutely accurate. Editors turn to free-lancers whom they know because they recognize that they will be getting dependable research. The true professional will never submit an article if he has the slightest question about the accuracy of any detail in it. Editors also know the professional writer will meet deadlines.   —*Amelia Lobsenz*

Get a Big Desk

Looking for ideal writing conditions? Then get as big a desk as possible; a flat door or a slab of plywood is fine. When my notes and research materials are spread out beside the typewriter, there never seems to be enough room.

Use a flip-over desk calendar with a page for every day. It's great for jotting down your day's schedule, telephone numbers, names and addresses. Every few weeks you can look through the calendar and see what projects remain undone.

Keep a file cabinet for clippings. This may not pay off immediately, but in time the clippings will become more and more valuable and save you hours of time in the library.   —*Robert Gaines*

Corporate Books: Fertile Field for Writers

One field of writing which has been mined only on the surface is the research, writing and editing of books for business, industry and related organizations. The closest most corporations come to preparing a book is to assign a lone writer, independently, to write a company history to commemorate, say, the fiftieth anniversary. Looking at the project realistically as well as creatively, there is absolutely no reason why the result should be a dull, plodding chronological history that never gets read and which turns out to be a costly promotional white elephant. You have only to turn to another type of corporation—the university—to see what kind of books can result when the corporation is attuned to producing works that are, to a large extent, meaningful.

There is an old saying that "every man has a book in him." Paraphrasing this, "every corporation has a dozen books in it." But they have to be developed. Management has to be sold on the idea and it has to be convinced that it is neither going to rattle a good many skeletons in the corporate closet nor divulge competitive business secrets.

Writers who are so inclined might do well to examine this field and undertake methods of selling businesses on the idea of doing books. There is no formula for obtaining assignments of this type. It takes selling and determination, as well as writing ability. Many writers find this kind of selling process painful. But the ones who are willing to persevere may end up with some good solid assignments.

Writers in this field, however, must be willing to *collaborate*—not only with the sponsor of the book or members of the company's management staff, but often with several researchers, another writer or editor. Sometimes the very selling of such a book requires the labors of an editorial team, rather than an individual writer. Therefore, in making an approach, a writer should sound out other people who might be required for this kind of teamwork effort, to be prepared to tell the would-be client just what kind of talent he can bring to bear on the assignment.

Have a Walk-In Closet

When I designed my office space (14 x 20 feet) I included plenty of book shelves and such refinements as acoustical ceiling and recessed lights. But the most important single feature was the walk-in closet included in the plan. I recommend it highly as a morale factor in any such office plan. All I have to do to make my office look neat is close these big double doors. (The doorway is six feet wide and equipped with suspended folding doors.) In the 4 x 10 feet space behind these doors are all my file cases, photo files, unsightly shelves of large brown envelopes holding research materials, office supplies—even field clothing and fishing tackle.

—*George Laycock*

Better than One

Some years ago, during a visit to New York City, I fell in with a cheery fellow by the name of Wilbur Cross III who was always, he said, on the lookout for contacts in foreign places with whom he might work. I thought no more about it and flew back to Scotland.

About three months later the same Cross wrote me a most eccentric letter asking me for 2,000 words on the State of Scottish Humor (incidentally, the most dismal subject on which I have ever written). I got a small check. Since then my file of correspondence with Will has grown to more than an inch thick and we have collaborated on 20 or 30 subjects. For example, I pick an idea out of a British magazine, say a cutting about how Cleopatra's Needles reached London and New York, send it across and he touts it around various New York editors, perhaps getting a go-ahead. So I produce some more material from British libraries and he does the same in New York and eventually sends me a draft of what he's done. I add a little and Anglicize the laughable Anglicisms he's tried to insert and send it back and, with luck, we each get a check.

Sometimes it's less than successful and the brilliant idea fails to attract the proper amount of editorial interest, so we share between us any losses incurred on expenses. But of course the idea is still in the files and it is only a matter of time before one of us gets hold of a perceptive editor by the ears and rubs his nose properly in it and then we are all set again.

In round figures, a good idea ought to be worth 20 per cent, the research 30 per cent, the writing 40 per cent and the selling 10 per cent. So the idea and research would be justly rewarded by half the takings and it is on this split that we work, regardless of each author's actual contribution. Man-powered flying, the great bookie swindle, a Berlin escape story—all these and more came from germinal ideas which developed into good stories once they had been chucked across the Atlantic Ocean a few times. Multiple authorship may sound strange and it certainly takes a little getting used to at first. But it does bring to print, or at least to the stage of the final draft, all sorts of themes that might otherwise have fizzled out in the hands of only one person. And when you get your $250 check for a $500 article, it is no moment to think "Why, I could have done the whole thing!" Better, instead, to reflect that half a loaf is better than no dough.   —*J. A. Maxtone Graham*

Saving Thoughts and Ideas in a Daybook

I keep a kind of daybook. Into it everything goes—business data, expense accounts, events of the day which can be mined for articles and other information. For example, here is an entry for last September which says, "Met an old gentleman on the train who says the doctors have given him only three weeks to live. Says he is trying now to get to the roots of a great many questions he never had time for before — not necessarily religious; often related to people; to what he has really thought of them."

The daybook might even record valuable statistical data suddenly come upon; or the name of a local newspaper somewhere which has such a flavor of Americana that it's worth a subscription; or a provocative authority, encountered socially, who would make a good subject for a future interview.   —*Ardis Whitman*

Keep Alert to Reprint Revenue

You can increase your chances for reprint revenue by taking the initiative. If you think you have something for *Reader's Digest,* send them a carbon as soon as the first magazine has your piece definitely scheduled. Then send a proof and, if still no word, the article as it appears in print. *Science Digest* is a market for the secondary rights of articles in the popular science field. Consult *Writer's Market* subject index for other markets.   —*Tom Mahoney*

Three-by-Five-Inch Record Keeping Cards

I keep track of queries and manuscripts out, payment due and other matters by noting each on 3 x 5-inch cards and keeping these and story subjects in a recipe-sized box. I always know where everything is and who owes me what.   —*Alfred Balk*

Always Line Up New Work Before the Old Runs Out

I have always felt that the first secret of making a living in the magazine article writing field lies in the word "flow." Article ideas, go-aheads, finished manuscripts—they must all flow constantly. There must never be a dam-up anywhere along the line. If there is, the result could be a major loss of income.

A man who makes buttons would never never allow himself to end a production schedule without having another order to start upon the next day. Yet, article writers time and again finish one assignment only to find themselves without another job to begin. Regularly they find themselves without even an idea for another piece. They must now start from scratch calling the editor, outlining a suggestion, waiting for a go-ahead. This takes much time and slashes deeply into income.

It may be difficult to interrupt a piece while one hunts ideas for the next, but this compartmentalization of the mind is essential to maintain flow. I have done this for years and, thus far, I have never ended a piece without having at least one other upon which to begin. Sometimes I have a dozen and I worry like the dickens about how I am going to manage; but I suspect that this kind of tension is infinitely more desirable than the kind you get when you don't have a job to do.   —*Lester David*

A Writer Needs an Office

Does a writer really need an office? My answer: a resounding "yes." For more than 15 years I've maintained an office away from home. It is a place of unbroken concentration—a place to work.

A writer's office needn't be fancy. It does, however, need to be fairly spacious. My own office, in a preferential business neighborhood in Los Angeles, is divided into four rooms: (1) a small outer reception area where, incidentally, I display some of the books and magazine articles I've written (the article display is updated monthly); (2) a mailing alcove — which puts immediately at hand all the necessities for mailing manuscripts; (3) a library—which in my case runs to some 15 four-drawer filing cabinets and shelving space for the rather vast library of magazine back issues I've built through the years; (4) and, finally, my own "working" office, which is air-conditioned.

Here, in privacy and without interruption, I can work efficiently. Here come my story contacts (people who perhaps would feel uncomfortable visiting me at home) and, as often, story subjects themselves, for I conduct many interviews in the office.

But foremost, I think, is the simple fact that nothing spurs a writer to writing more than does an office. When he leaves his house he is on his way "to work." When he arrives at the office, he is "at work." The demarcation is clean and clear. Plain or fancy, an office for the professional writer is a place of work—writing.

—*James Joseph*

Spare Time Writing: Research and Interviews

Writing articles in your spare time, especially when you have an unrelated full-time job, is difficult. You can't leave your post in midmorning, for example, to interview someone. Nor can you tell your employer you will not be in for a week because you must go out of town to obtain material for an article.

As a freelance writer who holds down a regular 9-to-5 position, I have tried to lessen these difficulties by limiting my article ideas to those for which research and interviews can be done in my own community or, at most, within a radius of an hour or two of travel.

I find lunch hours fine for quickie visits to libraries and other facilities near my office. Such visits are extremely productive when I know exactly what I am looking for. This I accomplish following a preliminary visit simply to check what references are available and spot exactly where they are located.

A lunch hour does not offer enough time for a satisfying personal interview. I leave interviews and involved library research for evenings and weekends. I have found that many individuals do not mind being interviewed during the evening or on a Saturday or even Sunday afternoon. They are flattered that a writer is interested in what they have to say and usually are quite cooperative. Many persons prefer to chat informally while relaxing at home rather than in the hectic atmosphere of their offices. When they realize my own predicament of finding time as a spare time freelancer, they are usually eager to be helpful.

Another device I've found useful, though it doesn't work all the time, is to attempt to interview people by mail. If a number of individuals are involved and the subject is the same, a simple questionnaire usually draws enough of a response to provide me with the quotes and material I need. Sometimes I send out a short provocative letter, written to arouse the recipient enough to respond with an extensive letter containing all of the pertinent quotes and information I want for my article.   —*William Kitay*

Convenient Office Keeps One in "Writing Position"

I work in an enclosed porch in the rear of the second floor of my home. It is small but I find this an advantage. My phone is within reach on a small stand to my left. Behind it are my files, two four-drawer cabinets. I have a draftsman's table to the right which I find handy for piling things on as well as for organizing my articles which I develop first on 3 x5-inch cards before approaching a typewriter. Bookcases are to the right and rear. I have coasters on my chair, as well as on my typewriter table—which is in the center of the room. When I need something, I rarely get up—I simply slide from one side of the room to the other. This keeps me continually in a writing position; on the seat of my pants. It also makes me sound like a very lazy man except that when I'm through writing I go out and run five or ten miles on the beach.   —*Hal Higdon*

Some Tips for Newspaper People
Who Want to Write for Magazines

My own route from newspaper to freelance writing was: all the beats, then columning, then the itch to do something a little more notable and make some money, a season of syndicate writing, an unsuccessful try at fiction (most reporters just aren't fictioneers) and, finally, all kinds of magazine stuff winding up in other national periodicals. (The bread-and-butter money is made in your steady production for the $300-$500 markets, pieces that will readily sell somewhere else if the first editor doesn't take them.)

Spend a year with the syndicates and Sunday magazines before you try full scale magazine writing. Reason: you get used to querying, acquire broader knowledge and experience with interviewing, learn to organize a piece and, importantly, find out your own best methods for working. Meantime, you get a stimulating flow of small checks. Markets? Use the published lists or *Editor and Publisher Yearbook*. I've done best with North American Newspaper Alliance (NANA) and King Features-Central Press, Cleveland. There are plenty of others.

And remember, always query. Reporters often ask me about queries. The main thing is to know a lot about your story first and have something special to offer on it to make it your exclusive property. Then just write a letter telling what you have, how many words it could run, one or two sharp anecdotes, the picture possibilities and how soon you can submit it. Don't ask for expense money or even discuss price unless you know the man personally. You'll be treated all right.

But the main thing a newspaper pro has to learn is that a good newspaper story is not necessarily—and, in fact, is *seldom*—a good magazine article. They're entirely different; different approach, surprisingly different methods of reporting, organizing and writing. You'll have no city desk to catch your mistakes, so be doubly certain on each fact and name. And don't think you can just go out and get your story, then sit down and knock it out free style and fast as you might do to make the bulldog edition. Contrarily, magazine articles are well researched, reported in depth and constructed one block upon another—after which you write and rewrite, cut and add and edit until maybe you've done the thing half a dozen times, especially your lead and conclusion.

John Bartlow Martin once told me that on his great material for *The Saturday Evening Post* about the Joliet prison, he spent at least

an hour with each of 80 prisoners, had many other sidebar interviews and spent about three weeks organizing before he did his first
draft. (It is worthy of note that Martin started as a reporter on the
Indianapolis Times and there's a tale that the then managing editor
didn't think John would ever quite make it as a reporter.)

Usually when I've explained to ambitious reporters about this
writing-in-depth bit, they either abandon the freelancing idea immediately or ask, "How do you ever find the time?" Answer: you
just find it. It may be time you don't spend at Harry's or the hour
after quitting time or the good old day off. You find it and you'll have
fun with it, too.   —*Charles W. White*

Keeping Track of All Activities on a Single File Card
It has always been my basic belief that the successful freelance
writer is one who has a number of projects going simultaneously,
some in the thinking or researching stages, some in the writing or
selling stages. Many years ago I evolved a rather simple (to me!)
device for keeping track of my projects and for being able to find, at
a glance, my general working position.

I take a 5 x 8-inch file card and rule it into six vertical columns.
These are headed: *Ideas to Query; Queries Out; In Research; In
Writing; Ms. Out;* and *Due.* Under the appropriate column I jot
down a "slug" for each idea or story. While I may have a whole file
of clips or notes with story ideas in a desk drawer, I put down under
the first column those ideas which I think are worth looking into
first and doing queries on. When a query is sent out, that "slug" is
moved to the next column along with the initials of the magazine it
went to and the date. Thus: Schools—Redbk—1/10/81

If I get an assignment, that article is entered under the "in research" column. When I finish research and start to write, the slug
moves along. When the piece is finished and mailed, it moves along
to the next column, again with name of magazine and date sent.
When it is accepted, the price is—hopefully—entered in the final
column, which gives me a bird's-eye glance of how much money is
coming in to me.

I have also taken to making two shorter columns at the bottom of the file card where I list ideas for book or other major projects and where I can keep track of important business mail, so that I know how long a letter to an editor or a research subject has been unanswered.

This may sound cumbersome, but actually it is quick, simple, clear; the cards need to be redrawn only every month or so, when there are a lot of hen-tracks on them. The bird's-eye picture I get of my whole situation helps to clarify things for me—such as, what shall I work on next, when did I send that piece to XYZ magazine and, look at all the money people owe me (or don't owe me).

I keep this card Scotch-taped to the flat pull-board under the top of my desk. One can while away many precious hours looking at it, thereby avoiding doing any of the work scheduled on it.

—*Norman M. Lobsenz*

Cost Accounting Your Time

Keeping a record of the way he spends his time helps a writer determine how to spend it most profitably in the future. Too often, however, a writer who does not keep such a record has no idea whether a given article or project was worth the time put into it. This is particularly true when several writing projects overlap.

My method is to write down at the end of each day what fraction of the working day went to which project. I consider the working day as one unit, whether it was a seven-hour day or nine hours. If the day was spent on several projects I record the fraction of the day spent on each, using a one-word code to designate the project. The smallest time unit noted is one-eighth of a day; most often the units are marked in whole days and half days, sometimes in quarter days. Professional work that cannot be fairly allocated to any one project, such as general correspondence with an editor or agent, is marked "Miscellaneous," meaning it was time worked but not allocated to any one project. About 30 per cent of all my working time is under this heading.

When a writing project is finished and paid for, I divide the total number of days spent on it into the dollars collected and so learn whether I can afford to put my time in this way for this kind of payment. In one case, $500 earned in three days' work (which was spread over a week or two) was worthwhile; in another, $500 earned for 15 days' work spread through six weeks was obviously a losing proposition.   *—Alden Todd*

Special Tips from a Columnist
The pace and spirit of a column should appear colloquial, somewhat loose and casual. I try to keep the writing in my monthly column (*Good Housekeeping's* "Speaker for the House") concise and non-repetitious, so it must be written and rewritten to achieve conversational effect with a minimum of words. The reason it must be tight is the limitation of space and the fact that I try to touch on eight or more topics per month. A daily or even weekly column can be more discursive. In fact, some daily columns chat on about only one subject each day.

I don't pay for contributions I use. Most people like to see their ideas in print and they write hoping to be quoted. These letters I edit freely, trying to make the writing bright, more literate and the ideas sharper. When I use quotes from a reader, I give only the town from which he or she comes—no names. This gives sufficient "credit" and avoids trouble. Now and then something comes to me which is obviously a submission, hopefully for pay; these I return explaining that I don't buy material from the outside.

A column, unlike individual articles, needs to build a following. This raises special problems. One trick is to have some continuing features, causes or subjects to which you return now and then. It's also important to specialize, to fence off some area as your field. Give and take is helpful, so you get readers writing to you by creating a friendly and intimate air, by quoting from letters, by specifically inviting comment.

No matter what type column it is, you must know what you are talking about and maintain accuracy. You must be completely honest. It's a big plus to be newsy and informative; readers learn that they will see something in your column before they see it elsewhere or that you'll explain it or fill in background. This puts them "in the know." Use wit and humor. Try to cover enough material of immediate or current concern to your readers so they may quickly identify and participate.

I have found the use of a different picture of me every month appeals to readers. The final decision of whether or not to use the writer's picture is, of course, up to the managing editor and art director. From my experience I can say that using a picture is valuable to a column. Its worth is multiplied if the picture is changed frequently. Readers feel they know me. They write about the pictures— the cat I'm holding, the chair I'm sitting in, even what I'm wearing or my hairdo. One standard picture used repeatedly can do this but to a lesser degree, as it tends to become too familiar to the reader. In my case, the pictures are taken in large lots by a photographer who is sent by the magazine to my home where I can be natural. The selection of pictures to run is made by the art editor.

Because of the wide-ranging area covered by my column, I keep hundreds of manila folders, one subject to a folder. Into these go ideas, clippings, news releases, sources, letters from readers, even phrases or possible headings I've jotted down. I also keep a folder for each month, so columns that are seasonal or timely swim up when needed. Since a single item frequently could find a place in more than one folder, it's important to make notes with a cross-reference. Better yet, use a copying machine to duplicate the item and file in more than one folder.   —*Charlotte Montgomery*

Don't Spurn a Specialty

When I first started freelancing after several years as editor of a baby magazine, I tried to avoid being typecast as a child development writer. Nevertheless, I kept getting assignments in that field. In learning to live with it, I've found that a specialty can offer many lucrative writing opportunities in addition to magazine pieces (of which I've had 50 in ten years). For example: service-type advertisements (at a five-figure fee for writing one a month); booklets (one

has hit 4,000,000 copies); TV commercials with a service introduction.   —*Ruth Newburn Smith*

Research that Pays Off
One day, several years ago, as I signed an initial five-figure book
contract, I happened to glance at a receipt on my desk. This receipt
—for $10—covered a four-month subscription to a leading daily
newspaper in Honolulu, a city that lies 2,000 miles from my office.
Yet, that $10 (a modest investment, surely) had, just as surely,
been multiplied many hundreds of times in the contract I was sign-
ing. Nor was that all. A major magazine had already agreed to condense the book—as a book-length article—even before the book
was written.

Obviously, my book subject was more than ordinary. No, I
hadn't simply "stumbled" (as some writers like to say) onto such an
extraordinary subject through sheer good luck.

A writer makes his own "luck" and what helps are newspaper
subscriptions such as the one I'd taken from Honolulu. From that
$10 subscription had stemmed my "good luck."

Whenever I'm planning a trip, I subscribe to the leading papers
in the cities or areas where I'll be. In fact, seldom a month goes by
that I don't jot out a small check (larger than the $10 of years ago
but still reasonable in terms of the potential payoff). One month I
may subscribe to a paper in Phoenix, Arizona. The next to one in
Salt Lake City. The next, perhaps to one as distant (working from
Los Angeles as I do) as Edmonton, Alberta.

Newspaper subscriptions—even if only a month of daily and
Sunday papers from a single city or area—give a writer an intimate
feel of fertile new story grounds. And they are rich in story leads
which never appear in major metropolitan newspapers of New York,
Chicago, Miami or Los Angeles.

What I'm saying is this: hundreds of major magazine story subjects of national interest are to be found in America's grass roots—
in its smaller, less story-hunted towns, villages and counties. Most of
these are missed and go unresearched and unreported by big-city

writers who read only the big-city papers (or such national papers, say, as the *New York Times, Wall Street Journal* or *Christian Science Monitor).*

Almost as many big-city stories are missed by big-city writers. They're missed by magazine writers who live and work in the very cities (and areas) to whose papers I so habitually subscribe.

My investment in "subscription research"—as I debit it on my accounting ledgers—has never failed to repay its cost many times over.

My not-by-chance subscription to the *Honolulu Advertiser* was typical. By September I knew that over the Christmas holidays I would be in Honolulu. Admittedly, I was already "over-assigned": I'd lined up six article assignments in Honolulu, work enough to turn a "holiday" into a considerable profit. Obviously, I wasn't looking— in subscribing to that Honolulu paper—for just an ordinary magazine or book subject. I was, as always, on the lookout for the extraordinary; for a story so compelling and so dynamic that it would be worth investigation when I was in Honolulu, regardless of the press of other assignments.

In a word, I was hunting a bonanza.

During the next three and a half months, that Honolulu paper came daily across my desk. Reading between the lines of its news stories (as one must), I spotted a few potentials, but none really as good as I was after. Then, just 10 days before I was to leave for Hawaii (it was early December now) a story appeared in the Honolulu paper that I knew instantly was "it"; a big, big story subject. Once in Honolulu, I quickly contacted the story's subject and, after a few hours of interviewing, confirmed the diagnosis I'd made from a distance of 2,000 miles. Here was one of those rarest of literary commodities—a "natural" true-life story. Yet, it had been missed as a magazine and book potential not only by a dozen top writers living in Hawaii, but by the newsman on the *Honolulu Advertiser* who'd reported it for his paper. Where his work left off, mine was just beginning. You see, my newfound (but not found by chance) story subject had lived a once-in-a-lifetime adventure. On the spot we negotiated and signed a contract. And, once back in Los Angeles, I put to paper (in outline form) the bonanza I'd found. Within two weeks a major magazine had agreed—even before a book had been written or, in fact, I even had a contract to write one—to condense the "book" as a magazine book-lengther. A month later came the book contract. I'm hopeful that Hollywood will eventually put this book on film—once it has been run as a magazine condensation and after it has been syndicated to a world-wide market. (Who knows but what the *Honolulu Advertiser* may be one of the syndicated buyers!)

And all this came from a $10 investment—from a newspaper subscription (daily and Sunday, by mail) which, as hundreds like it in which I've invested over the years, proved, as always, to be lined with gold.

Planning a trip? Before you buy your plane ticket, rush off a subscription check to the leading newspapers in the cities or areas you'll visit. Debit those dollars to "subscription research." You'll be glad you did.   —*James Joseph*

Ten Legal Dos and Don'ts for Writers*

1. *DO* be sure your arrangement with the publisher, producer or whatever is correctly reflected *in writing*—either a written contract, a letter agreement or, at the very least, a legend on the back of a check.

2. *DON'T* rely on "the law" for determining what your rights are, or on "the custom of the trade" or "what everyone knows." The *fact* is that the *law* is that you are considered to have conveyed whatever rights you and the publisher (or producer, or whatever) intended you to convey and, in the absence of a clear written understanding, the seeds of controversy and confusion are manifold.

3. *DO* try to arrange in writing for the copyright on your work to be in your name. While it is true that the nominal copyright owner

---

* These are general guidelines. In connection with any specific problem, consult your own attorney.

is not necessarily—or even usually—the owner of all rights in the work, it helps you to establish what rights you have retained if the copyright is in your name.

4. *DON'T* assume that because you are writing a factual work you can refer freely to living persons by name without risking a violation of their rights of privacy. While, with some exceptions, this used to be "the law," recent cases suggest that even a factual account about living persons may be held to violate their "privacy rights," e.g., if the account is "substantially false," if it is "fictionalized," if it probes "intimate" matters, etc.

5. *DON'T* regard yourself as a libel expert. If what you have to say about living people may hold them up to "hatred, contempt, shame or obloquy," have your lawyer review the work—and advise you as to possible changes, as well as what defenses may be available to you for that particular work.

6. *DON'T* regard yourself as an obscenity expert, either. The law in this field is changing very rapidly and if you are dealing with a subject matter which may "appeal to prurient interest," go beyond "contemporary standards of community mores" and be accused of having "no redeeming social importance," let your lawyer appraise the danger for you and advise accordingly in the light of the latest gyrations of both federal and state law.

7. *DO* bear in mind that "freedom of the press" is still one of our "first"and basic freedoms so that while it's wise to check with your lawyer, by and large, the United States Constitution and tradition is on your side.

8. *DON'T* rely on any rule of thumb when it comes to using quotations from other copyrighted sources. There aren't any rules of thumb—such as 24 lines or 2 verses of a song, or the like. In each case, the question is whether the nature and purpose and extent of the use makes it "fair." In that connection, whether the work using the quote is competitive with the work from which the quote is taken is very important. Remember, too, that "research" has been defined

as "plagiarism from two or more sources," which is much less likely to get you in trouble than plagiarism from one source.

9. *DON'T* throw away your notes, correspondence or manuscripts pertaining to a particular work. In addition to being invalable to you if you are sued for libel, copyright infringement, privacy, or anything else, you may need them to substantiate your tax deductions for business expenses. Moreover, you can make them the subject of gifts to educational, scientific or charitable organizations and get tax benefits for the gifts as charitable contributions.

10. *DO* do some tax planning *in advance*. You can, in advance, convey all or part of your interests in a work to someone you support who may be in a lower tax bracket than you; under the law, you can "average;" you can "spread forward;" and, of course, if you live abroad, there are many other possibilities as well. Remember that take-home pay is more important than gross dollars earned.

—*Harriet F. Pilpel*

ABOUT THE AUTHORS

Bernard Asbell, a former president of the ASJA, is author of nine books, several about important political figures, and contributes to many major magazines.

Carl Bakal writes chiefly on contemporary social and other problems for magazines such as *Harper's, Saturday Review, Reader's Digest, McCall's, Redbook,* and *Good Housekeeping.*

Alfred Balk, former reporter on the *Chicago Sun-Times,* is a full-time freelance contributor to *The Saturday Evening Post, Harper's, Reader's Digest, McCall's,* and others.

Erwin A. Bauer, author of *How to Catch Fish* and *The Bass Fisherman's Bible,* writes outdoors and adventure articles for such magazines as *Outdoor Life, True, Field & Stream,* etc.

Joseph N. Bell has written for most major magazines, i.e., *Reader's Digest, The Saturday Evening Post, This Week, True,* and *Harper's,* and is the author of seven books on sports and space.

Robert Bendiner, a contributor to leading American journals, is a former correspondent for the *New Statesman* (London), a Guggenheim Fellow, and author of *White House Fever* and *Obstacle Course on Capitol Hill.*

Theodore Berland, a Chicagoan and specialist in medical articles, is author of *The Scientific Life* and has written for *Reader's Digest, The Saturday Evening Post, Family Weekly,* United Features and *Redbook.*

Joseph P. Blank is noted for his human-interest narratives in many national magazines including *Look, McCall's, Pageant, Redbook, Reader's Digest, The Saturday Evening Post,* and *True.*

Murray Teigh Bloom, a founder and past president of the ASJA, has freelanced since 1940 and written more than five hundred magazine articles for every major U.S. periodical, plus the bestseller *The Trouble With Lawyers.*

The late **David Boroff,** associate professor of English at New York University, was a prolific contributor of articles, essays, and reviews to *Harper's, The New York Times Magazine, Saturday Review,* etc., and author of *Campus USA.*

The late **Ruth and Edward Brecher** together wrote some two hundred articles during the past quarter-century for America's foremost mass-circulation magazines.

Frank Cameron, writer for *The Saturday Evening Post, Reader's Digest, Life,* and other magazines, specializes in books about business, e.g., *Cottrell: Samaritan of Science* and *Hungry Tiger.*

Myron Cope is a contributing writer for *The Saturday Evening Post,* and has written for *True, Sports Illustrated,* and *Sport.* He is coauthor with Jimmy Brown of *Off My Chest.*

Robert Crichton, author of *The Great Imposter* and *Rascal on the Road,* specializes in "exploiting bizarre, ironic, and pompous personalities."

Wilbur Cross, author of eight books and hundreds of articles in the fields of history, biography, business, and industry, belongs to the Overseas Press Club, the Authors League, and the International Institute of Arts and Letters.

Lester David, of Woodmere, N.Y., has contributed more than five hundred articles to most of the top American publications, and has written biographies of Senator Edward M. Kennedy, Joan Kennedy, and Pat Nixon.

Beth Day is a contributor to major magazines, domestic and foreign. She has written five children's books and ten trade books.

Robert Deindorfer has written on many subjects, among them espionage and sports, for top national magazines. He is the author of eight books.

Allan W. Eckert, writer for *True, The Saturday Evening Post, Reader's Digest,* and others, is author of *The Great Auk, A Time of Terror,* and *The Silent Sky.*

Lawrence Elliott covers Alaska and Canada for *Reader's Digest.* He is also author of *A Little Girl's Gift* and biographies of George Washington Carver and Senator Daniel K. Inouye.

Stanley L. Englebardt is a freelancer with nine nonfiction books, a television documentary, and over five hundred published articles to his credit. He specializes in science subjects.

Paul Friggens, formerly a roving editor for *Reader's Digest,* is coauthor of *The Black Hills* and visiting lecturer at the University of Colorado.

Robert Gaines, associate editor of *Family Weekly,* writes on sports, personalities, and travel for many magazines, including *Cosmopolitan, Pageant, Catholic Digest,* and the *Herald-Tribune Sunday Magazine.*

Robert Gannon has written on science and natural history for *Reader's Digest, Popular Science, Mechanix Illustrated,* and *The Saturday Evening Post.* He is author of *The Complete Book of Archery* and six other nonfiction books.

Milton Golin, publisher/editor of a number of medical journals, has written for *The Saturday Evening Post, Reader's Digest,* and *Today's Health,* and wrote *The Business Side of Medical Practice.*

Arturo F. (Arky) Gonzalez has written more than seven hundred magazine and newspaper articles, a book on the politics of suburbia, and is presently consultant to the United Nations.

J.A. Maxtone Graham, a Scottish writer (and ex-farmer), lives in England and writes for *Sports Illustrated, Esquire* "and anyone who'll have me," on any subject but politics and medicine.

Mary Anne Guitar has contributed to *McCall's, The New York Times Magazine, Mademoiselle,* and *American Home.* Her books include *Twenty-Two Famous Artists Tell How They Work* and *The Divorce Handbook.*

Max Gunther, a former *Time* editor, has freelanced since 1956. His main output is for *The Saturday Evening Post* and *True,* plus occasional short fiction and books.

Dickson Hartwell, contributing editor to *The Arizonan,* has written for *Reader's Digest, This Week,* and *The Saturday Evening Post.* He is author of *Dogs Against Darkness* and coeditor of *Off the Record.*

Arthur Henley, an ex-radio and TV writer, has contributed to *McCall's, Pageant, The New York Times Magazine, Saga, Argosy, This Week,* and *The Saturday Evening Post* and is the author of five books.

Nat Hentoff, staff writer for *The New Yorker,* is associate editor of *Liberation* and contributing editor to *Stereo Review.* His books include *Jazz Country* (a novel), *The New Equality, Peace Agitator,* and *The Jazz Life.*

Booton Herndon, author of twelve books, has written for most major magazines including *Nation's Business, Reader's Digest, Redbook, The Saturday Evening Post, Esquire,* and *True.*

Hal Higdon, author of *The Beginner's Running Guide, The Union vs. Dr. Mudd,* and nine other books, writes for many major magazines under his own name and "Lafayette Smith."

The late **Al Hirshberg** wrote for *Look, Life, Reader's Digest, The Saturday Evening Post, Good Housekeeping, McCall's,* and *Redbook* and is the author of *Fear Strikes Out, Prodigal Shepherd,* and twenty-three other books.

Morton M. Hunt is author of *The Natural History of Love, Her Infinite*

Variety, and numerous articles for *The New Yorker* and other magazines. His specialty is the behavioral sciences.

Edward Hymoff is the award-winning author of four books and writer of more than a thousand magazine articles on aerospace science, military and international affairs, and other topics.

Theodore Irwin, erstwhile magazine editor (*Look,* etc.) has written some five hundred magazine articles, six nonfiction books, and two novels. His specialties include health, social problems, education, and investigative reporting.

James Joseph has written on adventure, business, science, aviation, and other subjects for nearly every major magazine. Among his many books are *Float Free* and *Here Is Your Hobby.*

Ray Josephs, former foreign correspondent, is author of twelve books and hundreds of magazine articles. His *How to Gain an Extra Hour Every Day* has been published around the world.

Bern Keating, who specializes in travel, French, and Southwestern U.S. history, has written for *Holiday, National Geographic, Playboy,* and *Reader's Digest.* Fluent in French and Spanish, he is also a professional photographer.

William Kitay, writer on health, medicine, and social problems, is author of the medical career guide *Challenge of Medicine.* His book *Overcome Arthritis* has been published in the U.S. and in six foreign translations.

The late **John Kord Lagemann** specialized in personalities, psychiatry, and medical and social problems for such magazines as *Redbook, McCall's, Reader's Digest, This Week, Cosmopolitan, Popular Science, Parents,* and *Esquire.*

George Laycock has written on outdoors and conservation subjects for *Better Homes and Gardens, Today's Health, Argosy, Field & Stream,* and *Sports Illustrated.* His six nature books include *Sign of the Flying Goose* and *Never Pet a Porcupine.*

William J. Lederer, author of *A Nation of Sheep, All the Ships at Sea,* and *The Ugly American* (with Eugene Burdick), has written for many magazines including *The Saturday Evening Post, Reader's Digest, Ladies' Home Journal,* and *Esquire.*

The late **Hannah Lees,** author of many books and articles on human relations, also wrote fiction.

Edward Linn, a contributing writer for *The Saturday Evening Post,* is author of *Veeck as in Wreck, The Last Loud Roar,* and *The Hustler's Handbook.*

Amelia Lobsenz, who has her own public relations firm, has written two hundred articles for national magazines and three books, one of which was a Junior Literary Guild selection.

Norman Lobsenz, 1965 president of ASJA, has written more than two hundred articles for *Reader's Digest, Redbook, McCall's,* and *Good Housekeeping.* He is the author of twelve books, including *Anatomy of Love* and *No-Fault Marriage.*

Tom Mahoney's articles on business, science, and medicine have run in virtually every major magazine. His six books include *The Story of George Romney* and *The Great Merchants.*

George McMillan has contributed pieces to *Good Housekeeping, Holiday, Life, The Saturday Evening Post, Sports Illustrated,* and most of the other major publications.

Eve Merriam has written for *Ms., The New Republic, The New York Times Magazine, The Saturday Evening Post,* and *Saturday Review.* Among her many books is *Growing Up Female in America.*

Keith Monroe, contributor to *The New York Times Magazine, The New Yorker, Boys' Life,* and *Reader's Digest,* has written for magazines since 1946 and is author of ten books.

Charlotte Montgomery, *Good Housekeeping*'s "Speaker for the House," also has written columns for *Redbook, Lifetime Living,* and *Tide* and is a lecturer.

Neil Morgan writes about the contemporary American West, is a columnist for the Copley newspapers and author of six books, among them *California Syndrome.*

Terry Morris, former president of ASJA, has been published in virtually all writing media and specializes in human-interest "as-told-to" stories for such magazines as *Redbook* and *McCall's,* and is the author of six books.

Don Oberdorfer is a national correspondent for the *Washington Post* and magazines including *The Saturday Evening Post, Life, Reader's Digest,* and *The New York Times Magazine.*

Vance Packard is best known for his books on contemporary America: *The Hidden Persuaders, The Status Seekers, The Pyramid Climbers, The Waste Makers.*

Harriet F. Pilpel, a New York City attorney, has contributed to the *Atlantic, Harper's,* and *Publishers Weekly.* She is coauthor of several books, including *Rights & Writers* and *A Copyright Guide.*

Vernon Pizer, author of *Shortchanged by History,* and seven other books, has written for *The Saturday Evening Post, Reader's Digest, Esquire, This Week, Nation's Business, Ford Times,* and *American Legion Magazine.*

Charles Remsberg, who specializes in current affairs, crime, and social problems, has written for *Playboy, Good Housekeeping, Esquire, The New York Times Magazine, Reader's Digest,* and *True.*

Sid Ross, roving correspondent for *Parade* magazine, specializes in documentaries and exposés.

Charles Samuels has written book-length "autobiographies" of Ethel Waters, Buster Keaton, and Boris Morros, and biographies of Clark Gable, Tex Rickard, and other celebrities.

The late **Beatrice Schapper** contributed to *Reader's Digest, Redbook,* and *Today's Health,* lectured in New York University's Magazine Article Workshop, and was coordinator of NYU's "Dialogues with Editors."

Jose Schorr writes on law for the layman and is a contributor to a variety of magazines and syndicates.

Flora Rheta Schreiber, award-winning psychiatric writer, also does political profiles. Her books include *Your Child's Speech,* a biography of Sargent Shriver, and the bestseller *Sybil.*

Ruth Boyer Scott has written on science, health, and other topics for *Better Homes and Gardens, Family Circle, Glamour, Nation's Business, The Saturday Evening Post,* and *Today's Health.*

Arthur Settel, special assistant to the U.S. Commissioner of Customs, edited *This Is Germany* and wrote the book *One Year of Potsdam.* He has contributed to *Saturday Review, Tatler, Commentary,* and *Pageant.*

Ruth Newburn Smith, who specializes in child care and general reporting, writes for *Better Homes and Gardens, Charm, Family Circle, McCall's, Pageant,* and *Parents.*

The late **Edith M. Stern** wrote on psychiatry, gerontology, and children for *Reader's Digest, Parents, Redbook,* and *McCall's.* Among her books are *You and Your Aging Parents* and *Mental Illness: A Guide for the Family.*

Bill Surface is author of *Freedom Bridge* and *My War with Baseball,* plus many articles for such magazines as *Reader's Digest, The Saturday Evening Post, Life, Look,* and *McCall's.*

Frank Thomas does profiles and industrial, medical, and general reporting for many magazines, including *Reader's Digest, This Week, Catholic Digest, American Mercury,* and *Family Weekly.*

Alden Todd's books include *Finding Facts Fast* and *Abandoned Justice on Trial.* He is adjunct assistant professor, New York University, and has written many articles, speeches, and newsletters.

Alvin Toffler, author of *Future Shock* and *The Culture Consumers,* has published articles in *Fortune, Horizon, Saturday Review, The New Republic, Reader's Digest,* and many other magazines.

John R. Tunis has written hundreds of books, articles, and stories over the years to the delight of several generations of readers.

William Lynch Vallee's articles on movies, TV, radio, public relations, and other topics have run in *Cosmopolitan, Redbook, The New Yorker, Saturday Review, American Legion, Good Housekeeping,* and *Writer's Digest.*

Gerald Walker, assistant articles editor of *The New York Times Magazine,* was for six years a freelance writer for many major national magazines and president of ASJA in 1962.

A.M. (Art) Watkins's articles on housing have appeared in *Harper's, The Saturday Evening Post,* and the leading shelter magazines. He also writes fiction and drama.

Marvin Weisbord's articles on the social sciences and public affairs have run in thirty magazines. He is author of *Campaigning for President: A New Look at the Road to the White House.*

The late **Mort Weisinger** published two hundred articles and was also editor of "Superman." His paperback *1,001 Valuable Things You Can Get Free* has sold two million copies.

Charles W. White, former editorial page editor of the *Indianapolis Times,* has written articles and editorials for leading magazines in the U.S. His specialties include economics, education, and family life.

Ardis Whitman's many articles on psychology, philosophy, and religion have appeared in *Reader's Digest, Glamour, Ladies' Home Journal,* and *The New York Times Magazine.* Her books include *Meditation: Journey to the Self.*

James H. Winchester is a general-assignment reporter who has worked for *Reader's Digest,* CBS, G.P. Putnam's Sons, *The New York Times,* King Features, *Family Weekly, Boys' Life, True,* and other magazines.

Morton Yarmon, author of nine books and frequent contributor to national magazines, writes mainly on personal finance and job guidance.

Maurice Zolotow's many books and articles include a biography of Marilyn Monroe, several novels, *Stage Struck: The Romance of Alfred Lunt and Lynn Fontanne,* and *Shooting Star: The Life of John Wayne.*

BIBLIOGRAPHY

The list of reference sources below is a general one, designed to help those who are writing on a broad range of subjects. It is arranged according to the steps that a writer might follow in drawing up a research plan for a given piece of work.

There is no such thing, of course, as a standard, or "complete," list of reference books, because there are an endless number that writers can turn to for source material. No matter who compiles a reference collection, it can always admit additions, provided money and shelf space permit.

The items marked with an asterisk are priced low enough to justify a writer's considering buying them for handy use at home. The others are higher-priced and most writers will prefer to use them in a library.

To find specialized libraries, and special collections in general libraries:

American Library Directory (R.R. Bowker Co.)
Directory of Special Libraries and Information Centers (Gale Research Co.)
Subject Collections. Lee Ash, ed. (Bowker)
Special Libraries Association membership directories in various metropolitan regions, e.g., New York, Los Angeles, etc.

To find reference books, and books by subject:

Guide to Reference Books. Eugene P. Sheehy, ed. (American Library Association)

Reference Books: A Brief Guide. M.V. Bell & A.E. Swidan, eds. (Enoch Pratt Free Library)
Subject Guide to Books in Print (Bowker)

To find periodical articles:

Readers' Guide to Periodical Literature (H.W. Wilson Co.)

For research in specialized periodicals:

Applied Science and Technology Index
Art Index
Biological & Agricultural Index
Business Periodicals Index
Education Index
General Science Index
Humanities Index
Index to Legal Periodicals
Social Sciences Index

To find newspaper articles:

The New York Times Index
The Wall Street Journal Index
Index to The Times (of London)
The New York Times Obituaries Index

To find collections of unpublished papers:

A Guide to Archives and Manuscripts in the United States. Philip M. Hamer, ed. (Yale University Press)
National Union Catalog of Manuscript Collections (Library of Congress)

To find organizations and their resources:

Encyclopedia of Associations (Gale)

To find biographical information:

American Men and Women of Science (Bowker)
Current Biography (Wilson)
Directory of American Scholars (Bowker)
Who's Who in America and other directories published by Marquis
   Who's Who, Inc.

For information on federal government:

The Congressional Directory

To find periodicals in a given field of interest:

Standard Periodical Directory (Oxbridge). Includes U.S. and Canadian.
Ulrich's International Periodicals Directory (Bowker). Includes periodicals of all countries.

For information on various branches of the publishing industry.

Books: *Literary Market Place* (Bowker)
Magazines: *Magazine Industry Market Place* (Bowker)
Newspapers: *Editor & Publisher International Year Book* (Editor &
   Publisher)

To find which companies manufacture which products:

Thomas Register of American Manufacturers

For information on newly developed computer and microform information sources and systems:

Special Libraries (Special Libraries Association, monthly)
Microform Review (quarterly)

General:

World Almanac. The detailed index makes this the handiest one-
   volume reference source for a wide variety of facts.

Statistical Abstract of the United States. A compilation by the U.S. Department of Commerce of many kinds of statistics of interest to business.

Finding Facts Fast. Alden Todd (Ten Speed Press). A book of research methods.

INDEX

Other Writer's Digest Books

Market Books
Artist's Market, 474 pp. $11.95
Craftworker's Market, 570 pp. $12.95
Fiction Writer's Market, 504 pp. $15.95
Photographer's Market, 549 pp. $12.95
Songwriter's Market, 400 pp. $11.95
Writer's Market, 917 pp. $15.95

General Writing Books
Beginning Writer's Answer Book, 264 pp. $9.95
Law and the Writer, 240 pp. $9.95
Make Every Word Count, 256 pp. (cloth) $10.95; (paper) $6.95
Treasury of Tips for Writers, (paper), 174 pp. $6.95
Writer's Resource Guide, 488 pp. $12.95

Magazine/News Writing
Complete Guide to Marketing Magazine Articles, 248 pp. $9.95
Craft of Interviewing, 244 pp. $9.95
Magazine Writing: The Inside Angle, 256 pp. $10.95
Magazine Writing Today, 220 pp. $9.95
Newsthinking: The Secret of Great Newswriting, 204 pp. $11.95
1001 Article Ideas, 270 pp. $10.95
Stalking the Feature Story, 310 pp. $9.95
Writing and Selling Non-Fiction, 317 pp. $10.95

Fiction Writing
Creating Short Fiction, 228 pp. $11.95
Handbook of Short Story Writing, (paper), 238 pp. $6.95
How to Write Best-Selling Fiction, 300 pp. $13.95
How to Write Short Stories that Sell, 212 pp. $9.95
One Way to Write Your Novel, 138 pp. $8.95
Secrets of Successful Fiction, 119 pp. $8.95
Writing the Novel: From Plot to Print, 197 pp. $10.95

Category Writing Books
Cartoonist's and Gag Writer's Handbook, (paper), 157 pp. $9.95
Children's Picture Book: How to Write It, How to Sell It, 224 pp. $16.95
Confession Writer's Handbook, 173 pp. $9.95
Guide to Greeting Card Writing, 256 pp. $10.95
Guide to Writing History, 258 pp. $9.95
How to Write and Sell Your Personal Experiences, 226 pp. $10.95
Mystery Writer's Handbook, 273 pp. $9.95
The Poet and the Poem, 399 pp. $11.95
Poet's Handbook, 224 pp. $10.95
Sell Copy, 205 pp. $11.95
Successful Outdoor Writing, 244 pp. $11.95
Travel Writer's Handbook, 274 pp. $11.95
TV Scriptwriter's Handbook, 322 pp. $11.95
Writing and Selling Science Fiction, 191 pp. $8.95
Writing for Children & Teenagers, 269 pp. $9.95
Writing for Regional Publications, 203 pp. $11.95

The Writing Business

Complete Handbook for Freelance Writers, 400 pp. $14.95
How to Be a Successful Housewife/Writer, 254 pp. $10.95
How You Can Make $20,000 a Year Writing: No Matter Where You Live, 270 pp.
(cloth) $10.95; (paper) $6.95
Jobs For Writers, 281 pp. $11.95
Profitable Part-time/Full-time Freelancing, 195 pp. $10.95
Writer's Digest Diary, 144 pp. $12.95

To order directly from the publisher, include $1.25 postage and handling
for 1 book and 50¢ for each additional book. Allow 30 days for delivery.

For a current catalog of books for writers or information on *Writer's
Digest* magazine, *Writer's Yearbook*, Writer's Digest School correspondence courses or manuscript criticism, write to:

Writer's Digest Books, Department B
9933 Alliance Road, Cincinnati OH 45242

Prices subject to change without notice.